Outsiders

Also by Laure-Anne Bosselaar

Night Out: Poems about Hotels, Motels, Restaurants, and Bars, coedited with Kurt Brown

The Hour Between Dog and Wolf

Outsiders

Poems about Rebels, Exiles, and Renegades

Edited by Laure-Anne Bosselaar

MILKWEED
EDITIONS

Published 1999 by Milkweed Editions
Printed in the United States of America
Cover design by Adrian Morgan, Red Letter Design
Cover art by Simone De Sousa
Interior design by Donna Burch
The text of this book is set in Minion.
99 00 01 02 03   5 4 3 2 1
First Edition

The epigraphs on p. xxiv are from: Charles Simic, ["Always the foreigner . . ."] from *Oprhan Factory* (Ann Arbor, Mich.: University of Michigan Press, 1998), 95. Copyright © 1998 by Charles Simic. Reprinted with permission from the University of Michigan Press; and Stanley Kunitz, "An Old Cracked Tune" from *Passing Through: The Later Poems, New and Selected* (New York: W. W. Norton, 1995), 21. Copyright © 1995 by Stanley Kunitz. Reprinted with permission from W. W. Norton and Company, Inc.

The quote on p. xix is from Richard Hugo, "On Hearing a New Escalation" from *What Thou Lovest Well, Remains American* (New York: W. W. Norton, 1975), 53. Reprinted with permission from W. W. Norton and Company, Inc.

Milkweed Editions is a not-for-profit publisher. We gratefully acknowledge support from the Elmer L. and Eleanor J. Andersen Foundation; James Ford Bell Foundation; Bush Foundation; Dayton's, Mervyn's, and Target Stores by the Dayton Hudson Foundation; Doherty, Rumble and Butler Foundation; General Mills Foundation; Honeywell Foundation; Jerome Foundation; McKnight Foundation; Minnesota State Arts Board through an appropriation by the Minnesota State Legislature; Creation and Presentation Programs of the National Endowment for the Arts; Norwest Foundation on behalf of Norwest Bank Minnesota, Norwest Investment Management and Trust, Lowry Hill, Norwest Investment Services, Inc.; Lawrence and Elizabeth Ann O'Shaughnessy Charitable Income Trust in honor of Lawrence M. O'Shaughnessy; Oswald Family Foundation; Piper Jaffray Companies, Inc.; Ritz Foundation on behalf of Mr. and Mrs. E. J. Phelps Jr.; John and Beverly Rollwagen Fund of the Minneapolis Foundation; St. Paul Companies, Inc.; Star Tribune Foundation; and generous individuals.

Library of Congress Cataloging-in-Publication Data

Outsiders : poems about rebels, exiles, and renegades / [compiled by]
    Laure-Anne Bosselaar. — 1st ed.
        p.   cm.
    Includes index.
    ISBN 1-57131-409-1 (pbk. : alk. paper)
    I. Alienation (Social psychology)—Poetry. 2. American poetry—20th century.
3. Marginality, Social—Poetry. 4. Social isolation—Poetry. 5. Dissenters—Poetry. 6. Exiles—
Poetry.
    I. Bosselaar, Laure-Anne, 1943-
PS595.A4097 1999
811'.54080353—dc21
                                                                        98-32217
                                                                        CIP
This book is printed on acid-free paper.

For Brown, Mathieu, Maëlle, and Maureen

Special Thanks

For your warmth, friendship, confidence, editorial savvy, and for championing this anthology with such faith, my deep gratitude to you, Emilie Buchwald.

For selflessly recommending long lists of poems by students, friends, fellow poets, and for their warm support of this project, thank you Kim Addonizio, Dorianne Laux, David Rivard, and Valerie Duff.

Thanks, Fred Courtright, for helping me with the permissions process, digging up those impossible-to-find addresses and other acknowledgment information.

To the Warren Wilson community of writers: I would be an outsider without you.

Outsiders

AL YOUNG

Foreword

We have just enough religion to make us hate, but not enough to make us love
one another.

—Jonathan Swift, *Gulliver's Travels*

My own earliest memories of what it feels like to be an outsider date
back to age seven, when my twenty-two-year-old mother sent me and
my infant brother, Richard, back to Mississippi to live with her older
sister's family in Laurel. Because our father, like millions of other
southerners, had emigrated with us from Mississippi to Detroit to-
wards the end of World War II to find work that would pay enough to
raise the family's standard of living, I already knew what it was like to
be the new kid on the block. Recalling the film imagery of that period,
I felt as though I had been parachuted into alien territory: not only
was it crucial that I overlook the hard landing; if I was going to make a
place for myself in the hardscrabble pecking order that extended from
block to school to playground, I had to hit the ground running.

One windy afternoon, five years old and still new to Detroit, I was
sprawled on the ground, a small wooden stick in each hand. I was
doing what a lot of kids still do with toys and or those tiny, round-
headed Fisher-Price wooden people: I was playing with those sticks as
though they were characters in a play that was unfolding in my head.

"All right now," one stick was telling the other, "you do that again,
and we might have to fight a duel."

"Oh, yeah?" said the other stick. "We'll see about that!"

And while this little drama was unfolding, with much clashing of
sticks and with grunts and groans and crashes and screeches pouring
from the lips and throat of their spellbound ventriloquist, I was jarred
by some unscripted laughter. Looking up, I saw a much older boy of
fourteen or fifteen, one of the neighborhood bullies.

All three of us froze—Good Stick, Bad Stick, and I, the noisy puppet master.

"What you doin?" the bully asked.

"What's it look like? I'm playin."

"Playin, huh? Then you must be crazy."

"No, I ain't crazy. I'm just playin."

"And that's what you call playin? Sittin up here talkin to yourself. Who you talkin to, boy?"

"Leave me alone. This is a game I play."

"Oh, yeah? Well, I ain't never heard tell of nobody playin no game where they be sittin up with sticks, talking to theyself. And don't come gettin smart with me, boy, I can get crazy, too. I'll smack you upside your head."

The instant Bully Boy reached for me, I was on my fleet feet, whizzing towards home. And could I ever haul ass! A born racer, I would later run track. I was a fiery wrestler, too, though no match for a kid twice my age. He dogged my tracks right smack to the front door, where my mother just happened to have been looking out the window. I was home free.

"Don't you ever lay hand on this boy again," my mother told him, "and don't ever let me hear of you touching any of my kids."

"I ain't bothering him none," the sucker lied, squinting his evil eyes at me.

After he was gone, I broke into tears.

"What are you crying about?" Mother asked.

"Mother, am I crazy?"

"What *are* you talking about?"

"That boy told me I was crazy."

"What were you doing for him to tell you something like that?"

"Playing. I was making, acting like some sticks I had were people and I had 'em talking."

"Yes," she said, "you always have done stuff like that. Don't tell me that's how come he was chasing you."

"I guess he thought it was all right to pick on me 'cause I wasn't like everybody else."

"Lemme tell you something," my mother said, "that boy don't look to me like he's got a drop of sense himself. I can't think of anybody I know that isn't at least a little bit crazy. I know I am."

Now I knew I would really have to stay out of Bully Boy's way for sure, which I managed to do. And I was pleased and oddly impressed with my younger brother Franchot, whose temper flared faster than mine, when a month later he threw a rock at this bully, who had tried to terrorize Franchot, too. Not only did Franchot throw that rock; he took dead aim and hit his target head-on. The kid came to our front door with his scalp bloodied and his own mother in tow. I watched from inside the house while our two mothers went one-on-one in an abusive verbal confrontation.

By the time I was sent back south to live, by turns, with my Aunt Doris and Uncle Cleve in the bustling mill and cannery town of Laurel, and with my grandparents on their forty-acre farm in Pachuta, I was already a pretty good paratrooper. I knew a lot about the outsider game of Us and Them.

Growing up during the McCarthy Era, I quickly came to understand that, by and large, people experience and subdivide the world in terms of Us and Them. In this ever-shifting yet reliably fixed worldview, now elegantly invalidated by science, every last one of us is someone else's Outsider. My undergraduate days at the University of Michigan in the Dark Ages of the Cold War fifties, when professors and students discreetly policed their own political opinions and thoughts, quivered with that strangely romanticized (and largely fantasized) heroism the youth of one era transmits to youth who follow. As budding artists and intellectuals whose social attitudes had been warped by the very republic we did our best to rebel against, we tended to distrust or even dislike artists and intellectuals. But we might have acted up or acted out our resentment a lot more truculently had we known what the journalist-historian-novelist Herbert

Mitgang documents in *Dangerous Dossiers*, his 1988 book subtitled *Exposing the Secret War Against America's Greatest Authors*. Even today it shocks me to learn that for half the twentieth century the FBI, the post-war CIA, and other intelligence agencies spied on writers and other artists I admired. Mitgang's list included poets Carl Sandburg, Robert Frost, Stephen Spender, and Archibald MacLeish; novelists Ernest Hemingway, William Faulkner, William Saroyan, John Dos Passos, Thornton Wilder, Graham Greene, John Steinbeck, Rex Stout, Arthur Miller, Sinclair Lewis, Pearl S. Buck, Thomas Mann, Theodore Dreiser, Dashiell Hammett, Thomas Wolfe, Aldous Huxley, Ignacio Silone, Robert Frost, W. H. Auden, Edmund Wilson, Norman Mailer, and Truman Capote; playwrights Lillian Hellman, Tennessee Williams, and Arthur Miller; and artist Georgia O'Keeffe and sculptor Henry Moore. Even publisher Alfred A. Knopf—to my mind an insider if ever there was one—had not been spared, and neither will many of the contributors to this remarkable anthology that poet Laure-Anne Bosselaar has edited.

The celebrated, blacklisted singer-actor-orator Paul Robeson is perhaps best remembered for his portrayal of Othello, Shakespeare's tragic Moor, a classic outsider in Venice on professional assignment, who is tricked into believing that his Venetian wife, Desdemona, has been unfaithful to him. But the gifted Robeson, like thousands of others maimed or destroyed by the pernicious indictments of the House Un-American Activities Committee, died a broken man. Hounded by a democratic government that systematically persecuted its own citizens, cutting shockingly little slack for dissidents, Robeson, in his last days, could very well have quoted Othello: "I pray you in your letters, / When you shall these unlucky deeds relate, / Speak of me as I am. Nothing extenuate, / Nor set down aught in malice. / Then must you speak, / Of one who loved not wisely, but too well."

What Thou Lovest Well, Remains American, Richard Hugo's memorable 1975 book of poems, includes the startling "On Hearing a New

Escalation," whose concluding lines crackle with disarming political clarity:

> Killing's still in though glory is out of style.
> And what does it come to, this blood cold
> in the streets and a history book printed
> and bound with such cost-saving American
> methods, the names and dates are soon bones?
> Beware certain words: Enemy. Liberty. Freedom.
> Believe those sounds and you're aiming a bomb.

In those days when the fragile legacies of populism, the labor and socialist movements, the proletarian novel, and grassroots democracy were still afoot, we gobbled up Samuel Beckett, Alain Robbe-Grillet, Marguerite Duras and all the French writers of the so-called "new novel"; we took seriously the existential pronouncements of Jean-Paul Sartre, Simone de Beauvoir, Albert Camus, and Jean Genet, a straight-up criminal who, looking back, seems to have been setting the stage for the entrances of novelist and heroin-denunciator William S. Burroughs and, as decades unfolded, Eldridge Cleaver, legendary cofounder of Oakland's Black Panthers and best-selling author of *Soul on Ice*, not to mention all the writers who became autobiographers and crypto-novelists once implication in the Watergate scandal had made them famous; and we hugged and kissed such champions of the underdog as Nelson Algren, James Baldwin, LeRoi Jones, Jack Kerouac, and *Invisible Man*, Ralph Ellison's masterpiece of an outsider novel. And there was plenty of room left to digest two novels entitled *The Outsider*, one by Colin Wilson, and the other by Richard Wright, both of whose themes crisscross. Wright penned his existentialist novel about a shrewd, pathological outsider named Cross Damon after he had abandoned Mississippi, Chicago, and New York to settle in Paris, where he was befriended by de Beauvoir and Sartre, who confessed towards the end of his life that the grim fears of his childhood played a vital role in shaping his influential brand of atheistic existentialism. Like all the other writers I've mentioned in this paragraph, Sartre was an avid lover of jazz, a music that seems to thrive under Republican and other tight-lidded regimes.

And while we kids listened endlessly to Bird and Monk and Miles and Trane and Mingus, we couldn't help translating into philosophical (and, by extension, political) speculations every nuance of their personal eccentricities, which we had diligently or sloppily concocted from hearsay, articles, interviews, and wayward imagination. What kept us high was the brilliance of their deviance, the night-worlds they inhabited, and their trickster-genius for enabling hip listeners like Us to co-inhabit those anti-day worlds with Them. Those musicians were the ultimate outsiders: hip, unrespectable performing artists who played so gorgeously for us and for themselves from some glittering, dark beyond.

The phrase "beyond the pale," as it grazed my ears, always connoted something outside: something "out there," as jazz jargon still would have it, off to one side, separate but not necessarily so unequal as incomparable to, and certainly by no means subject to, the rules and measures and regulations that governed the chilling, official White world of the Eisenhower Era. For my generation, which was roughly the Civil Rights generation that came of age between the late 1950s and the mid-1960s, between the Beat Generation and Hippies, nuclear holocaust was taken for granted. We assumed that sooner or later the Bomb would be dropped (it didn't matter whether we dropped it on the U.S.S.R. or if they dropped it on us); it was a lose-lose strategy, a weapon that made no sense. Cartoonist Walt Kelly's Pogo Possum and Albert Alligator spoke for us when they said, "We have seen the enemy, and he is us."

Subtly or bluntly, we all understood that, sooner or later, we faced the absurd prospect of being annihilated, quite unglamorously, by an atom or hydrogen bomb. Thumbtacked to a friend's funky, low-rent wall was a poster you could buy that spelled it out. Boiled down, its instructions read: IN CASE OF ATOMIC ATTACK . . . PLACE YOUR HEAD BETWEEN YOUR LEGS, AND KISS YOUR ASS GOODBYE.

When the Industrial Revolution began to put the squeeze to eighteenth-century farm and village life, the theme of social and psychological alienation crept into Western literary fiction, where it has prevailed. At the close of the twentieth century, the alienated hero (and antihero)—the outsider, the outcast, the rebel, the "other"(at least for readers and scholars of so-called serious fiction)— has stolen the whole show.

It didn't seem to matter that physicists and other scientists, who had spent the better part of the century demonstrating the interconnectedness and interdependency of all things, all phenomena, on earth, were declaring that the very notion of "otherness" might turn out to be the grandest fiction of all.

To any thinking or even reasonably informed citizen of the twenty-first century, the dualistic concept of an "outsider" should seem absurd. You don't have to be "a scientific rocket"—as Danny Ford, ex-coach of the University of Arkansas football team, put it—to zero in on the connections that link a child laborer in Indonesia, a prisoner in Texas working the toll-free switchboard TV watchers ring to place their phone orders for that Asia-made product, and the bargain-hunters who dial up clutching their credit cards. At the housing compound the factory runs outside of Jakarta, this hard-working girl earns fifteen cents an hour cranking out cool shoes for joggers in the United States, Europe, South America, Japan. Perhaps she and the other girls who work with her dream of Hollywood love stories or tap their feet and sway to Michael Jackson, or Wu Tang, or one of America's biggest exports: Madonna.

Long before the findings and theories of chaos science and complexity science trickled down to lay readers, Alexander Pope— whose seventeenth-century empire-sanctioned religiosity might still seem corny or outdated to many modernists, post-modernists, and counter-culture professionals—struck a harmonically similar note in his enduring *Essay on Man:*

> Nothing is foreign: Parts relate to whole;
> One all-extending, all-preserving Soul
> Connects each being, greatest with the least;
> Made Beast in aid of Man, and Man of Beast;
> All serv'd, all serving! nothing stands alone;
> The chain holds on, and where it ends, unknown.

May the 170 "outsiders" whose insider takes on that experience in our epoch of instant "communication" remind us how lonely we are.

LAURE-ANNE BOSSELAAR

Preface

When I started editing *Outsiders* I had a very precise, methodical strategy in mind about how to find the poems, how the anthology would be structured (seven sections), and how those sections might inform each other to create a solid, engaging arc to the book.

Over one thousand poems were submitted and researched. With the flawless judgment and enthusiastic assistance of Valerie Duff, this number was brought down to 250. Many poets had more than one "indispensable" poem for this anthology: poems I could not *help* but publish. I selected, filed, copied, and started putting the first draft of the anthology together, section by section.

That's when I lost control of the book and it took control of me. None of my structuring ideas worked. Each arc collapsed. The poems—however I ordered them—refused any classification. Only then did I realize how naïve I had been: how could I even think of a plan to force outsiders *inside* anything! Wasn't "outsiderness" what this whole anthology was about?

Finally, I decided to adopt an alphabetical ordering by author. It seemed the only solution. Fortunately, this worked—except for those poets represented by more than one "indispensable" poem, which seemed to give them precedence over the rest. So again, I selected and ordered. And it was only when the present manuscript was assembled that the book felt balanced, whole, and—at last—democratically structured. To quote the last line of Jonathan Holden's poem, "Saturday Afternoon, October," the book could now express with confidence:

I'm on nobody's team.

Always the foreigner, the stranger, someone a bit fishy.
Even the smiling dummies in store windows eyed me
with suspicion today.

—CHARLES SIMIC, *Orphan Factory*

An Old Cracked Tune

My name is Solomon Levi,
the desert is my home,
my mother's breast was thorny,
and father I had none.

The sands whispered, *Be separate*,
the stones taught me, *Be hard*.
I dance, for the joy of surviving,
on the edge of the road.

—STANLEY KUNITZ, *Passing Through*

Outsiders

KIM ADDONIZIO

Broken Sonnets
(Volunteer Worker, Family Shelter)

for JS

1.
After supper in the big room,
the children are left to us.
I don't know what their parents do—
iron a shirt for morning, write letters, haunt the bus
stops hoping for change. A few stretch out
on bunk beds down the hall,
doze to radios. Someone screams *Shut*
your face, I'm sick. Someone makes a call
on the pay phone. The kitchen finishes up,
dishes tucked away, the long steel trays
slammed home. We pass out paper plates, bright-topped
jars of paint, the colors soon smeared to gray.
Fights break out over the brushes. A baby wails
unattended. More children come. More souls.

2.
Some torment the smaller ones,
hit them when we're not looking.
It's only after the astonished cry we turn
to comfort one child, scold the other. *I'll fucking*
cut you, Ramon tells me, jabbing a toothpick
at my eye. Then he drags it slowly
across his wrist like a razorblade. I stick
a gumdrop on the sharp end. *See?*
I say. We're doing sculptures tonight.
I take his toothpick from him, attach

it to the thing we're making. Later Lamar will fight
with Harold. Blanca will touch
her cheek where a hand mark blooms.
Squashed candies will litter the room.

3.
Why do I come here? To prove
I'm good? Mostly I feel helpless.
And God knows I don't love
these hours—the noise,
the near-disasters—the paint-drenched
hair, the toppling off a chair
kicked out from under. I hate the stench
of the bathroom, the brown soiled underwear
of some little girl whose name I don't know—
she's new—who cries for her mother
while I wipe her. I want to go
home to my own child. Some other
volunteer can take my place.
But all week I'm haunted by her face.

4.
This is the kingdom of purgatory:
dorm rooms and a cafeteria, an empty
gym upstairs, and three locked lavatories.
The first of the month is holy.
The door's bolted after ten at night.
And our prayers can't help—no one
here is going to heaven. An oversight
on God's part; it's nothing they've done,
just one of those mistakes even the Lord
isn't immune from.

But it's blasphemy to say so. Blame
Satan, then; say that God is good.
Or listen to the Buddhists: the universe is perfect as it is.
This is the kingdom that doesn't exist.

5.
Another fight. This time I'm caught
between them on the stairs. At the bottom, Elly
holds a wooden clog in one hand, about
to hurl it at Harold. He
stands on the landing with a milk crate raised
above his head. I get hold
of Elly, drag her off. Another worker says, *She's pissed
about being here again.* I ask Harold.
He says, *I heard her mama
got a job but fucked it up. There's eight
kids. And one born dead. Promise
not to say I told you. She hates
us knowin her business.* He smiles.
You okay, he says, *considerin you a white girl.*

6.
The children call my name, and keep saying it,
over and over, frantically, the way
I imagine Christ might pray,
glued to his cross, before he quit
believing God was anything but
some factory worker who'd made
sure the head was screwed on tight
before stamping his backside
with a copyright mark. *Help me, help me.*
They think I can unbreak the snapped crayons,

the dropped cookies, fix the seams tearing open—
I admire the purple flowers, the Christmas trees
around their houses, they always draw houses,
I'm there, I hold them, the wounds miraculously
almost close.

7.
Small moments of grace—they're supposed to be enough.
Or more accurately, all that is possible—
I can't change anything, not the tough
luck of being where they are, not the trouble
they've had or whatever's to come.
What I do is show up once
a week in their lives. Sometimes I try to write poems.
Which do nothing, and end in silence.
And which lie. The children are real,
they're not who I've made of them.
I guess I wanted you to listen—wanted you to feel
more, and maybe sadder. That girl in the bathroom,
who soiled herself: I invented her. The truth is this:
she is the child who doesn't exist,
the one God and the angels forgot. Or simply missed.

CONSUELO DE AERENLUND

Cuando el tecolote canta, el Indio muere*

* When the owl sings, the Indian dies.

Long before the Spaniards came
we would go down to the lake for water,
our *hiupiles* woven with jaguars
and sacred bats.
Braided wool coiled like
a serpent on our heads
to rest
the round-bellied *tinaja*
that smelled of good red clay.

After my moon came down upon me
a boy stared as we passed
on the mountain,
stared so hard that color came
to my face.
We did not speak. Custom was not so.
He followed me to the lake every day,
tried to catch the fringe of my shawl
and pull me to him. I snatched it away.

My sisters hid their giggles behind their hands.
Juan's eyes burned my bare arms and neck
until one day, according to custom, I took
my *tinaja* by both ears, raised it
above my head and smashed it on the rocks.
Water and shards pierced the air.
Now he took my hand
led me to his mother's house
and told her how it was between us.

Today the water jugs are plastic
light as pumice stone and striped
with gaudy colors, unbreakable.
Near fire they melt and smell like cheap tallow.
And what will my little sisters do
when it comes time to marry?
No shards will fly.
Waters will not scatter.
Then the owl will sing by day
and on soft, silent wings
cast a blackness over the face of the sun
while the empty eye sockets of our ancestors
slowly fill with tears . . .

NADYA AISENBERG

Leaving Eden

The date palm and the cypress
aspire to heaven
as do the peacock's lapis breast,
the fountain ascending.
The pious long to be buried
near Jerusalem's golden gate.
We pass through the bazaar hearing
the soft moan of the world mourning itself
with the silken banners
and flower-filled arches of holy words.

We are always and continually leaving Eden,
the nuzzling lips of the giraffe,
the garden where the heaped ambrosia lay.
                    Are these memories
or the desperate imaginings of exile? The body
straining backward for a glimpse of something
blooming in the sand:
                    our own mysterious selves
before we tasted *murder, mortality.*

JOAN ALESHIRE

The Double

Attractive at that distance, hair fanning out
thick, a bit frizzy, falling straight
but belled above her rough wool cape, she danced,
I thought, to entertain her friends:
passengers first in line for the bus.
Free of convention, constraint, she seemed
someone I might know or want to meet.

Then her palm turned up at the end
of her shrug. She moved close
as the front of the line winced,
and, as one, took a step back, as far
into the wall as it could go.
She threw her art against refusals
all up the row; in her cajoling mouth
I could see the dark hole where her teeth
should be, and the rash across her cheeks,
her pupils so blasted they seemed not to see
the upstate students giggling, imitating her
in their basketball jackets, collectively
shaking their heads, while the couple
in bowling shirts from Las Estelas Lanes
almost bowed, wishing not to offend.

I shrank, wanting the wall to take me
in, but the man and woman just ahead,
who seemed least advantaged among us,
alone found something to give, with soft advice
to *Get off the streets, child, get help*
child—As if she'd gotten all she needed,

the one who'd been begging left to our journey
all those who turned away, the two who truly
met her, and I terrified she'd notice
my odd-shaped arms and ask why I didn't embrace
and take her home, recognizing me:
her true, betraying sister.

ELIZABETH ALEXANDER

Boston Year

My first week in Cambridge a car full of white boys
tried to run me off the road, and spit through the window,
open to ask directions. I was always asking directions
and always driving: to an Armenian market
in Watertown to buy figs and string cheese, apricots,
dark spices and olives from barrels, tubes of paste
with unreadable Arabic labels. I ate
stuffed grape leaves and watched my lips swell in the mirror.
The floors of my apartment would never come clean.
Whenever I saw other colored people
in bookshops, or museums, or cafeterias, I'd gasp,
smile shyly, but they'd disappear before I spoke.
What would I have said to them? Come with me? Take
me home? Are you my mother? No. I sat alone
in countless Chinese restaurants eating almond
cookies, sipping tea with spoons and spoons of sugar.
Popcorn and coffee was dinner. When I fainted
from migraine in the grocery store, a Portuguese
man above me mouthed: "No breakfast." He gave me
orange juice and chocolate bars. The color red
sprang into relief singing Wagner's *Walküre*.
Entire tribes gyrated and drummed in my head.
I learned the samba from a Brazilian man
so tiny, so festooned with glitter I was certain
that he slept inside a filigreed, Fabergé egg.
No one at the door: no salesmen, Mormons, meter
readers, exterminators, no Harriet Tubman,
no one. Red notes sounding in a grey trolley town.

DAVID ALPAUGH

Herbie

was almost eighteen years old.
He loved to wear the kamikaze aviator's cap
his uncle had brought home from Guadalcanal
with the flap always dangling down under his chin
because somebody wasn't paying attention
or didn't know how to snap the buckle in.

One day Herbie asked if he could ride my
little red tricycle. I looked up and shook
my head, *"No."* Next thing I knew Herbie
was pedaling my trike up Mariners Place—
and I was sitting in the middle of the sidewalk,
crying for my mom and justice

while Howard and the other boys ran after Herbie,
throwing stones and calling him names—
like sparrows pestering a red-tailed hawk

though our big bird had barely spread his
wings before one of my pedals broke off
under the thrust of his size ten sneaker
and Herbie's Wild Ride was over.

This is my earliest memory:
a Mongoloid in an enemy aviator's cap,
pedaling up the street on a tricycle.

I remember the benign smile on his face
as he turned and looked back to let me know
it was nothing personal—just a matter of pure joy.

You can have my fucking tricycle, Herbie.

DOUG ANDERSON

Itinerary

In Arizona coming across the border with dope in my tires
and for months tasting the rubber in what I smoked.
With a college degree and a trunk full of the war.
Working in one place long enough to get the money
to stay high for a month and then moving on. Drinking a quart
of whiskey, then getting up, going to work the next day.
A little speed to burn off the hangover. In the afternoon
a few reds to take the edge off the speed, and then to the bar.
At the bar, the madonna in the red mirror. My arm around her
waist and the shared look that said, *The world is coming apart,
let us hold one another against the great noise of it all.*
Waking with her in the morning and seeing her older,
her three-year-old wandering in and staring with a little worm
of confusion in his forehead. The banner on her bedroom wall
that read ACCEPTANCE in large block letters.
At night going out to unpack the war from my trunk.
A seabag full of jungle utilities that stank of rice paddy
silt and blood. To remind myself it happened. Lost them somewhere
between Tucson and Chicago. Days up on a scaffold
working gable-end trim with Mexicans who'd come through
a hole in the fence the night before. Rednecks who paid
me better than them. Laughing at jokes that weren't funny
to keep the job. At a New Braunfels Octoberfest getting in a fight
with a black army private who wore a button that read,
Kiss me I'm German. Don't remember what the fight was about.
Back in Tucson. Up against the patrol car being cuffed
for something I don't remember doing. Leaving the state.
With Jill in San Antonio. Finding her in the same bar,
driving her home in her car because she was too drunk.

The flashers on behind me, then the flashlight in my face.
In those gentle days they drove you home. Stealing Jill's car
out of the impound lot next morning to avoid the fee.
Later sitting buck-naked across from one another at the breakfast
table wondering who we were. This woman who wanted to live
with a man who had dreams so bad he would stay awake for days until the
dreams started to bleed through into real time and he had to go back
the other way into sleep to escape them. Who woke with the shakes
before dawn and went to the kitchen for beer. Later walking down
to the barrio slowly, without talking, our hips touching.
The Mexican restaurant, a pink adobe strung with chili pepper
Christmas Lights the year round. Inside, the bullfight calendar
with the matador's corpse laid out on a slab, naked and blue
with a red cloth across his loins and the inevitable grieving virgin
kneeling at his side. The wound in the same place the centurion
euthanized Christ with his spear. Our laughing then not laughing
because laughter and grief are born joined at the hip.
An old Mexican woman fanning herself at the cash register,
her wattles trembling. *Recordar:* to remember, to pass again
through the heart. *Corazón. Corragio.* Core.

BOB ARNOLD

No Tool or Rope or Pail

It hardly mattered what time of year
We passed by their farmhouse,
They never waved,
This old farm couple
Usually bent over in the vegetable garden
Or walking the muddy dooryard
Between house and red-weathered barn.
They would look up, see who was passing,
Then look back down, ignorant to the event.
We would always wave nonetheless,
Before you dropped me off at work
Further up on the hill,
Toolbox rattling in the backseat,
And then again on the way home
Later in the day, the pale sunlight
High up in their pasture,
Our arms out the window
Cooling ourselves.
And it was that one midsummer evening
We drove past and caught them sitting
Together on the front porch
At ease, chores done,
The tangle of cats and kittens
Cleaning themselves of fresh spilled milk
On the barn door ramp;
We drove by and they looked up—
The first time I've ever seen their
Hands free of any work,
No tool or rope or pail—
And they waved.

ROBERT AYRES

Corporeal

In seventh grade Larry Saclarides had a gym locker next to mine, and dark skin, and dark hair. Thick black hair. My skin was light as beeswax; my legs, smooth as candles.

I started shaving in high school when peach fuzz wouldn't pass muster those early morning inspections.

In Animal Husbandry, I learned low testosterone accounted for nearly all my corporeal shortcomings: my fine bones, my slight musculature, my high-pitched voice, learning I demonstrated in lab when the calf I finally roped threw me time and again in the slick green shit.

I learned my kind are culled to keep these exact characteristics out of the herd . . . cut like the *castrati* for sopranos, sold by their parents for eunuchs, or suited for monastic life, illuminating manuscripts.

They failed though to blind us, failed to see how deep in a man's eye desire's root will grow.

JOHN BALABAN

Heading Out West

All evening, below a sprig of yarrow,
by creekwater plunging through willow roots,
a cricket preened its song in our yard.

Down by the back eddy spinning with whirligigs,
I watched a fox pause from lapping up water
to lift a delicate paw and scratch
at redmites itching the root of its ear.

Then, as the sun ignited the willow stand
a blackbird flapped off a branch,
crossing shadowy fields like a thought.

All evening as crickets called, I creaked
a rocker on our paint-peeled porch,
sipped whisky, watched mist and fireflies
fill up the meadow, and considered
—long before I was a father—
my fellow Americans, the funny business of being married,
my deadly job and the jobs that would follow,
and all I could think of as I sat there
—safe from harm, steadily employed, happily married—
was how to get away.
                    At morning, I left,
hopping a ride west on the interstate, past
the cauldrons of Pittsburgh, its choked air,
past HoJos, Exxons, Arbys, Gulfs,
in the yammer and slam, the drone of trucks,
past the little lives that always are there,
past locusts chirring in a Tennessee graveyard,
past kudzu, pecans, then yucca and sage,

past armadillos scuttling off the berm of the highway,
. . . all the while wondering just what I was doing,
not sure where I was going; less sure, why.
But standing there, hanging out my thumb,
squinting at the stream of oncoming cars.

RUTH ANDERSON BARNETT

The Anorexic

It's only the attic I miss.
No need to think of the bright kitchen
or the table buried in food.
It was always dusk in the attic.
I built the dolls' house
of cardboard and rags:
my dolls lived there where no one could see them.
They mustn't be seen,
each was missing a limb—an arm, a leg, obvious
though I'd done my best to disguise them.

Momma was always in the kitchen:
when I came in from school
she made me taste.
When Poppa got home,
he'd ask if I'd been a good girl.
But I had always failed at
something.

—

In the textbook,
the organs were all salmon-colored and waiting—
waiting for food, waiting for seed to grow.
That's where the hunger is.
I am here. And the hunger is there.
I went into the bedroom,
looked at my body in the full-length mirror
and I could see it was open.

—

Sometimes, boys circled around me
after class: I saw what they saw:
the black jersey
slipping from my left shoulder,
the tattoo of a heart there.
Once I met my lab partner below the grandstand.
I drew him there, my body
controlled him. But I never did it again—
my flesh stuck to his flesh,
his hands on my breasts,
searching for something.

———

One day when I was 5
I went into my father's study.
He looked up from his writing and smiled.
"Come over here, skinny,
let's see if you have grown,"
then, "Come on now, lift up your skirts."
I tucked my dress around my waist
and held it there.
When my panties were around my ankles,
he made me turn my back.
I shut my eyes tight.
I heard him say, "Ah."
My flesh puckered, it touched his fingers.

———

In philosophy class,
we were reading the *Symposium*.
"After the division

each desiring his other half,
they came together and throwing their arms
about one another, entwined
in mutual embrace, longing
to grow into one, on the point
of dying of hunger."
Sometimes I feel I'm dissolving,
like the time with the boy
under the grandstand, my body
going off, my body
fucking a boy without me.

———

After a while,
every time Poppa gave me a caramel
I said I would save it for later.
I put them in the toilet:
I flushed them down.
It made me sad to do it.
They stuck in my teeth,
I loved to suck them.
All I could think of
was the way he sat at the table
stuffing himself, his jaws
pumping up and down, up and down,
like their bed at night,
the springs creaking.
Later when he said I used to be pretty,
I said, "You just like fat women.
You can do what you please
with fat women."

———

Hunger—Incubus—Engrossing flesh—Disgusting—
there is something

flowing into me, into my mouth,
into the other mouth—

———

In my dream,
I'm under the grandstand,
crawling in mud, covered in mud.
I look up through the seats.
A brightness is there, in the heavens.
If I can touch it, it will be sweet.
But it is unfair, unfair—
Then I take off my body and drop it.
I stride onto the field,
my legs long and gleaming.
I spread my arms and brightness
bends down to me. A light with no wings.
It lifts me above the grandstand,
where cheers rise from the empty bleachers
again and again,
though I am like a cloud by now, like vapor.

ROBIN BECKER

The Crypto-Jews

This summer, reading the history of the Jews of Spain,
I learned Fra Alfonso listed "holding philosophical discussions"
as a Jewish crime. I think of the loud fights
between me and my father when he would scream that only a Jew
could love another Jew. I love the sad proud history
of expulsion and wandering, the Moorish synagogue walled
in the Venetian ghetto, persistence of study and text.
If we are the old Christ-killers on the handles of walking sticks,
we've walked the earth as calves, owls, and scorpions.
In New Mexico, the descendants of Spanish *conversos* come forth
to confess: tombstones in the yard carved with Stars of David,
no milk with meat, generations raised without pork.
What could it mean, this Hebrew script,
in grandmother's Catholic hand? Oh, New World, we drift
from eviction to eviction, go underground,
emerge in a bark on a canal, minister to kings, adapt to extreme
weather, peddle our goods and die into the future.

MARVIN BELL

The Book of the Dead Man (#58)

1. *About the Dead Man Outside*

They came to the door because he was small or went to some church
    or other or was seen in the company of girls or boys.
Well, he was small and went to synagogue and didn't know what to
    make of it.
They said he was from some tribe, but he didn't understand it.
They acted as if they knew what they were doing.
They were the executioners of brown eyes and brown hair, and he
    happened to have both.
Well, he said, and they went away before he awoke.
They were a dream he was having before he became the dead man.
Today the dead man lives where others died.
He passes the crematoriums without breathing.
He enters the pit graves and emerges ashen or lime-laced.
He shreds the beautiful tapestries of history and hangs in their place
    the rough shirts and dank pants forsaken at the showers, and the
    tiny work caps.
He mounts the hewn chips of shoe soles, the twisted spectacles, the
    tortured belts and suspenders, the stained handkerchiefs.
Here, he says, is history, maternity, inheritance.

2. *More About the Dead Man Outside*

Let none pardon the Devil lest he have to begin again.
Let no one weep easily, let no one build portfolios of disaster
    snapshots or record the lingo of the know-betters, let no one speak
    who has not considered the fatalities of geography.
The dead man does not suffer skinheads lightly, their evil is legion.
With an olive branch, he whips the villains into a frenzy of repentance.
The dead man tattoos the war criminals with the numbers.

The dead man wonders what America would be like if every war were a wall engraved with the names of the lost.

Well, they said, he was from some tribe or other, and he didn't understand it.

When the dead man was a dead child, he thought as a child.

Now the dead man lives that others may die, and dies that others may live.

Let the victims gather, the dead man stays on the outside looking in.

Let the saved celebrate, the dead man stands distant, remote.

The dead man listens for the sound of Fascist boots.

They will be going again to his grave to try to cut down his family tree.

This time the dead man will see them in Hell.

STEPHEN BERG

Nostalgia

Why look back at the old roads again? Drugs and buggery flourished. My grief took root. Why inspect each vice that started when thought dawned? It wounds the sky, drags me into the black future.

This is the last innocence, the last introverted peek into the reamed-out precincts of Hell, the last choral swoon. It's over—betrayals, disgusts, my effigies of a metaphysical unknown.

Who wants to hire me? What beast should I adore? What face of the divine defile? Whose hearts should I break? What lies should I defend? What blood should I wade through?

Avoid the police. Live poor. With a withered fist lift the coffin lids, sit until you evaporate. *Mon ami*, terror isn't French.

I'm so alone nothing about me rises above the paltry earth.

My punishment? To take one step after another, lungs frozen, head a blast furnace, my daylight eyes drenched with night.

Time duplicates us after death. Where? Will we really be the same?

Shoot me in the face or I'll jam this pistol into my raving mouth, jump under those wheels. . . . Oh, I welcome it.

BRUCE BERGER

Without

Friends my own age all have kids they can't wait
        To have me appreciate,
To uncle the shrill mouths, the obscene smells, the din
        That rends every conversation,
The heedless egos screaming to be fed,
        Never satisfied
With less than stardom, demanding of every encounter
        The sacrificial center
And winning with genetic snake eyes those
        Who had always been most close,
Friends whose mutually conspired futures
        Are undone by these
Fluke extrusions of their horny selves,
        Culling out their lives
And forcing an old confidant to be
        Kind to precocity,
A cooing extra or newly aloof,
        A chill uncaring self
Indifferent to a newborn's due attention—
        Having quaintly forgotten
How I scotched my parents' other plans?
        Training the nether lens
On foot-stomping tantrums in the proscenium
        I arched for strangers, I am
Whelmed by one tsunami of sympathy,
        Someone had to raise me.
Raising the matter of my own childlessness:
        Last of the Landers,
False lead among Bergers and destined no doubt

To draw the sum without
Subjecting my eye-rolling intimates
To speech's ugly roots
In my fresh whelp, next to stay up late
For his or her hot date,
To natter on my last back bumper ZEN
AND THE ART OF GRANDCHILDREN,
Clutching my freedom, trusting for surest friend
The quiet of a dead end.

ERIC BERLIN

Sea World

This lady in her wheel chair has been left
by whoever was pushing her, and has nothing
better to do than watch the tank where
the sharks float by. She leans on the rail
that guards the glass, her chin down like a punished child.
She didn't want to come out here, but here she
is at the end of her life with a purple
bag in her lap, face to face with a beast
whose mouth is propped open by its own teeth.
The two gold fish that somehow are still alive
move as slow as pennies dropped in a pool.

LAURA BOSS

When You Are Grown, Amanda Rose

When you are grown, Amanda Rose,
and fill out NEA forms
(if there still is an NEA in the
year 2024), you will check *minority*,
infant granddaughter, and
check the box *Hispanic* in that column
of minorities like flavors on a
Baskin Robbins ice cream list.
And at your first job interview your dark skin
will need no check mark when you are
sitting at some employer's mahogany desk
during this job interview—

And, perhaps, by then your father, my son,
will have told you how on his first trip
with your mother, a business trip to Australia,
your mother was not allowed to enter
a restaurant in Sydney when they stood at the entrance of
the gold damask draped room
because of the color of her skin
and how this also happened at the
next restaurant they tried, and the one
after that. And when my son went up to
the young owner of a Kosher restaurant
and the owner also did not want her to
enter, my son said that he was also Jewish
and how could this man discriminate after
how the Nazis had treated the Jews and the
owner replied "Please leave." And by then
my future daughter-in-law, your mother, was

crying and my son was both raging at the man
and falling in love with your mother though
who was to know that such discrimination would
spark the romance that would produce you, beautiful
Amanda Rose.
And how taxis passed them by,
this young couple holding suitcases,
he with his fierce green eyes and
her mascara streaking and her wild
dark hair forming curls around her angelic face—
her almost five foot frame looking so tiny next to him
(though he is just of average height).
And, finally, at the hotel the desk clerk saying their rooms were
not available because the previous occupants had decided
to stay longer and "to please try another hotel"
and how your mother cried all through that
"dream" trip according to your father
whose own shouting I have always found annoying
but your father yelled and yelled at that hotel manager with
threats of suits for discrimination until
the manager told the bellman to take
your mother and father's suitcases up to the
reserved rooms and your father first kissed your
mother and decided he was going to marry her.

And I also know that the sweetest, most gentle
voice I ever heard my son use was in the hospital
when you were born three months ago, Amanda Rose,
and he quietly said to you,
"You're going to have a good life."

AMY BOTTKE

How to Approach Your Lover's Wife

Spot her, but don't lock on her.
Walk toward her with shoulders back,

arms loose, confidently at your sides.
Shake hands with full eye contact.

Smile slightly, but do not grin or smirk.
Engage in conversation gradually, integrate

yourself into the group. Compliment her
on her belt, earrings, or broach

but not on intimate items—a ring,
her hair, a necklace. Say you know her

husband through his tennis club
or the soccer carpool. Do not bring up

her interests, though you know
her interests. If need be, tell her

you golf, read mysteries, belong
to a gym. Try not to focus on her

teeth, the corners of her mouth,
or her hands, though these things

might be difficult to avoid. Do not say
Robert tells me you voted

for the Republicans. Maintain status
of distant acquaintance. Laugh softly

at any joke told. Then sigh and stir
your drink. Look around the room.

Capitalize on any lull in conversation
by excusing yourself. Say you need

to freshen up your drink. Offer to fetch
anyone else a drink. Depart

without looking at her or him.
Change your drink to a double Stoli.

Move to the kitchen.
Chat recipes with the host.

LUCIE BROCK-BROIDO

Radiating Naïveté

I am a false philosopher of this
World, a steady congregation

Of one, nobody's panther, nobody's
Tinny cigarbox, nobody's violin, no

Midsummer naïf in Havana rain.
I am glad to see the summer dying

Off, the umbrage of the cornfields, breast-
High stalks gone brittle in the drought.

The headlights early coming on, dusk
Is an old adjective, color of the blind

Reading their prayer in pocks.
You should have been

A contender, a Canadian dime mixed
Up in our own, worthless & shiny, jamming

Up vending machines & roadside phones,
Old Indian. The harvest will

Be small this year & dear—
I'm nobody's truck farmer, nobody's juke,

Nobody's cold sweat on the wooden front porch,
Nobody's southern heartbreak hill.

I'm wide-eyed as Louis Armstrong when he woke
Moonlit in his darkened motel room: all

My white soprano injuries.
I am acquisitive, I pray

Alone. In the ashes, nobody's isotope,
No glass of milk. Nobody's stained-

Glass messages, not the radium
In its dish, wide-eyed

As Madame Curie, lit
By half-lives at her hand,

Nobody's sin, nobody's white-
Knuckled god, nobody's humming bird.

KURT BROWN

The Good Devil

He was bad at torture. Flubbed his first flaying.
Dropped his pointed trident
into a lake of oil and had to scorch himself
diving in to retrieve it. Came out looking
like a channel swimmer
sheathed in pitch. Once he stepped
on his own tail during a papal dis-
embowelment, dropped
the stomach of his Holiness
on the flagmarl, where it rolled into a nearby
flue. They had to fetch it out
with iron ropes and sticks.
And once, while the other demons drew
and quartered—neatly
splitting a false prophet like a chicken--
he was busy gazing off,
admiring the tapestry of fire
that flickered on the horizon.
He missed the special Days of Profanity,
the Blasphemers' Sabbath,
the millennial Parade of Pagans.
And when that poet showed up—
the Florentine with sallow skin—he was off
gathering teeth in the Betrayer's Oven
to polish and string for his mother.
The Gossips assembled, glad for work, tongues
humming like locusts
during the first Pharonic plague.
Rumor stretched its four necks and rose on leathery wings.

When the order came up
from below, winding its way through the bowels
of authority to ordinary drudges like him,
he was banished and had to hand in
his pitchfork, tines unbloodied,
shaft still immaculate of martyrs' grease.
He had to slouch in utter shame
through the Gates of Perdition into a new
and chastening light to make his living
by the sweat of his labor—
a poor farmer now,
condemned to delve in wet earth like a simple worm.
And everything he touched throve.
Everything he planted grew
in prolific, earth-nurturing rows
ready to be consumed,
glistening with everlasting life.

ANDREA HOLLANDER BUDY

Ellis Island, September 1907

Unless the officials could pronounce and spell a name,
every Eastern European Jew on the ship from
Rotterdam became a *Hollander.*

Sadie, who was only twelve, wrote each letter down:
Haych, she said as she wrote it,
Oh, Ell. She had two countries now:
the one rising ahead of her like leavened bread
and the one her father said had saved them
which now would name them.
Out with the bad, in with the good,
her mother said. *Ckollander*
she practiced saying, over and over,
new food in her mouth,
and dropped the name she was born with
like a baby's gummed zwieback.
She wrote it down again and again
trying it out like a bride-to-be, wondering
who she would become with a name like this
in this place
where she could become it.

HAYDEN CARRUTH

Little Citizen, Little Survivor

A brown rat has taken up residence with me.
A little brown rat with pinkish ears and lovely
almond-shaped eyes. He and his wife live
in the woodpile by my back door, and they are
so equal I cannot tell which is which when they
poke their noses out of the crevices among
the sticks of firewood and then venture farther
in search of sunflower seeds spilled from the feeder.
I can't tell you, my friend, how glad I am to see them.
I haven't seen a fox for years, or a mink, or
a fisher cat, or an eagle, or porcupine, I haven't
seen any of my old company of the woods
and the fields, we who used to live in such
close affection and admiration. Well, I remember
when the coons would tap on my window, when
the ravens would speak to me from the edge of their
little precipice. Where are they now? Everyone knows.
Gone. Scattered in this terrible dispersal. But at least
the little brown rat that most people so revile and fear
and castigate has brought his wife to live with me
again. Welcome, little citizen, little survivor.
Lend me your presence, and I will lend you mine.

CYRUS CASSELLS

Soul Make a Path Through Shouting

for Elizabeth Eckford
—Little Rock, Arkansas, 1957

Thick at the schoolgate are the ones
Rage has twisted
Into minotaurs, harpies
Relentlessly swift;
So you must walk past the pincers,
The swaying horns,
Sister, sister,
Straight through the gusts
Of fear and fury,
Straight through:
Where are you going?

I'm just going to school.

Here we go to meet
The hydra-headed day,
Here we go to meet
The maelstrom—

Can my voice be an angel-on-the-spot,
An amen corner?
Can my voice take you there,
Gallant girl with a notebook,
Up, up from the shadows of gallows trees
To the other shore:
A globe bathed in light,
A chalkboard blooming with equations—

I have never seen the likes of you,
Pioneer in dark glasses:

You won't show the mob your eyes,
But I know your gaze,
Steady-on-the-North-Star, burning—

With their jerry-rigged faith,
Their spear of the American flag,
How could they dare to believe
You're someone sacred?:
Nigger, burr-headed girl,
Where are you going?

I'm just going to school.

MARILYN CHIN

We Are Americans Now, We Live in the Tundra

Today in hazy San Francisco, I face seaward
Toward China, a giant begonia—

Pink, fragrant, bitten
By verdigris and insects. I sing her

A blues song; even a Chinese girl gets the blues,
Her reticence is black and blue.

Let's sing about the extinct
Bengal tigers, about giant Pandas—

"Ling Ling loves Xing Xing . . . yet,
We will not mate. We are

Not impotent, we are important.
We blame the environment, we blame the zoo!"

What shall we plant for the future?
Bamboo, sasagrass, coconut palms? No!

Legumes, wheat, maize, old swine
To milk the new.

We are Americans now, we live in the tundra
Of the logical, a sea of cities, a wood of cars.

Farewell my ancestors:
Hirsute Taoists, failed scholars, farewell

My wetnurse who feared and loathed the Catholics,
Who called out:

>   Now that the half-men have occupied Canton
>   Hide your daughters, lock your doors!

ELIZABETH CLAMAN

Show Biz Parties

My dad cracks a joke and two men laugh,
jiggling their scotch at a young blonde swathed in pink.
At the front door my step-mother smiles. *Darling.*

I am the girl in black velvet. Ten, eleven, twelve,
the years of black velvet. I curtsey and say, *Yes.*
Pour champagne. But as the house fills
      I become invisible.

Sitting on the stairs I watch an actor play piano,
a dancer kick her long leg over his head.
When Ty Power or Monty Clift passes, the crowd parts,
then closes. Women arch, eyes glitter for contact.

By two A.M., my dad licks champagne from a redhead's neck.
My step-mother's pale arms hug everyone.
The dancer yells, *Catch me!* and leaps on one man,
      then another.

Once in a while, late, women talk to me.
Drunk, maybe crying.

One night a woman holds up her little finger and says,
A prick this big—Why should I care?
When I wake up on the stairs, my step-mother's hissing,
You son of a bitch. And my dad keeps laughing.

In my room I slip out of my dress, smelling of scotch and smoke.
I watch in the mirror as I kick up my legs and shimmy,
my chest beginning to swell.

Naked in bed, I stroke my belly, and find the warm wet below
with my wrist. Beautiful Monty Clift, beautiful Ty Power.
     A prick this big. Beautiful.

DAVID CLEWELL

Poem for the Man Who Said Shit

At first I lost it in your beard
so I took a guess, told you the time.
You stepped closer and let it fly,
again and again, a single syllable,
a voice swollen with the confidence
that comes from years of study.
You gestured every way at once
like everything was part of some long story
you forgot all the words to but one.
By the time you waded into traffic,
your salvo booming louder,
I finally got it right and thought
why not, we all make what we know look easy:
high pressure systems, finite mathematics,
the impossible jumpshots we turn in our sleep.
And tonight if the filmclip makes the news,
a doctor will come on, swivelling
behind a sturdy desk, his mouth full
of polished stones like *childhood* or *the war*
or his favorite, *urban stress.*

If you're lucky down at the station
this won't take too long.
You go over and over your only story until
finally it could be anything, lost
on too many trips to the brain: *Lawnmower.*
Watermelon. The rookie cop is worried
he's losing his first bust.
The sergeant's been around, knows
even though he's got a family to think of
there's nothing he can do. When you leave,

he'll tell the rookie a long story,
how it's too bad the way the world is.
Me, I'm the witness who wouldn't swear
to anything. When I leave
the sergeant will say it's people like me.

LUCILLE CLIFTON

slaveships

loaded like spoons
into the belly of Jesus
where we lay for weeks for months
in the sweat and stink
of our own breathing
Jesus
why do you not protect us
chained to the heart of the Angel
where the prayers we never tell
and hot and red
as our bloody ankles
Jesus
Angel
can these be men
who vomit us out from ships
called Jesus   Angel   Grace Of God
onto a heathen country
Jesus
Angel
ever again
can this tongue speak
can these bones walk
Grace Of God
can this sin live

MICHAEL COLLIER

Robert Wilson

Though he is dead now and his miracle
will do us no good, I must remind myself
of what he gave, plainly,
and without guile, to all of us on the crumbling
flood-gutted bank of the Verde River
as we watched him, the fat boy,
the last one to cross, ford the violent shallows.
And how we provided him the occasion for his grace
tying his black tennis shoes to a bamboo fishing pole
and dangling them, like a simple bait,
out of reach, jerking them higher each time he rose
from his terrified crouch in the middle
of the shin-high rapids churning beneath him,
like an anger he never expressed.
And yet what moved us was not his earnestness
in trying to retrieve his shoes, nor his willingness
to be the butt of our jokes. What moved us
was how the sun struck the gold attendance star
pinned on the pocket flap of his uniform
as he fell head first
into the water and split his face,
a gash he quickly hid with his hands,
though blood leaked through his fingers as he stood
straight in the river and walked deftly toward us
out of the water to his shoes
that lay abandoned at our feet.

BILLY COLLINS

Going Out for Cigarettes

It's a story as famous as the three little pigs:
one evening a man says he is going out for cigarettes,
closes the door behind him and is never heard from again,
not one phone call, not even a postcard from Rio.

For all anyone knows, he walks straight into the distance
like a line from Euclid's notebooks and vanishes
with the smoke he blows into the soft humid air,
smoke that forms a screen, smoke to calm the bees within.

He has his fresh pack, an overcoat with big pockets.
What else does he need as he walks beyond city limits,
past the hedges, porch lights and empty cars of the suburbs
and into a realm no larger than his own hat size?

Alone, he is a solo for piano that never comes to an end,
a small plane that keeps flying away from the earth.
He is the last line of a poem that continues off the page
and down to a river to drag there in the cool flow,

questioning the still pools with its silver hook.
Let us say this is the place where the man who goes out
for cigarettes finally comes to rest: on a riverbank
above the long, inquisitive wriggling of that line,

sitting content in the quiet picnic of consciousness,
nothing on his mind as he lights up another one,
nothing but the arc of the stone bridge he notices
downstream, and its upturned reflection in the water.

PETER COOLEY

Brother Body

I.
Here I am, awakened by accident
in my motel room, called up by a wrong number
in a sacred place. Brother Body, me,
as St. Francis called his, surrounds the I,
naked the two of us, alone, cold,
this white sheet drawn up by the hands between us
before sleep, halfway home on a long drive,
the business done, here at a dump on the interstate.
If there is happiness, Lord, we can give ourselves,
it is this artless: the gratitude of waking,
my each breath corresponding to the first birds
drawing gold-leaf escutcheons at the window's edges,
the window's centers, the many centers, dark.
Together, You and I will fill them in.

II.
This body which was given me to wear
for a little while only, sits here in the diner
no one comes to anymore. It is five o'clock,
the first wash of evening traffic pouring down the street,
car lights strung on the darkening, dividing it.
The ancient waitress, as if preparing me for entrance
into my next life, has baptized me without asking,
calling me "Fred," whenever I stop off for coffee here.
And she blesses bread just by being so negligent
that the roll she brings is always broken.
I am fifty-three. Mornings now my left foot carries such a stiffness
I wonder what route it plans to take with me
in the decade ahead. We will not be together

forever, the flesh and I: when will we be divided?
Should I ask the waitress, priestess of my little rite?

III.
Mine, this body I will have to use to die
owning no other while I walk the earth
in anticipation of another walking.
Mine, too, how his ghost answers my stare,
7 A.M., standing before the mirror
wrapped in the shower steam I'm toweling off.
I think the years are gathering around the center
despite whatever push and pull I put it through.
I think I see the landslide I will enter, finally,
has begun its gravitational shift at belly, ass and thighs.
I do not think thinking can hold it back.
Now I'm draping the black towel around my neck,
but I'm no victor staring back at myself, grinning,
my grin a little grave Peter is hiding in.
What fun it will be looking back at this from the hereafter!
I plug in the shaver, lift myself to it. Now today.

WYN COOPER

Leaving the Country

for Larry Levis

He drifts into a room of strangers
who tell stories he thinks he's heard
though they seem different this time,
more lurid and real. He's never seen
these people before, who seem to know
when to use the right word, when to drop
their voices to whispers, to say
the last time he came into this room
is the last time he went anywhere
and the man wants out, now, but he
has to stay, no choice in the matter.

Each story takes the shape of a square
which works its way around him
until he's almost framed, then
he steps out, leaving a maze
of open squares all over the room
which itself is a square left open
at the door. He tries to shut
these voices from his mind, tries
to remember the great round world
outside these walls, the color
and fragrance of summer, the sky at dawn,

but all he can hear is the thunder
of voices around him, a dozen
stories at once, boxing him in.
He wants to give shape to a story

that will leave these people silent,
amazed, a story they'll tell
over and over, after he's gone.
His story will be about his leaving,
and they'll listen so carefully
they won't hear him go out the door
or run across the wet summer grass.

GERALD COSTANZO

The Old Neighborhood

for Gerald Stern

There was a time in my life when,
each evening after work,
I'd go down and sit in the bowling
alley. It was the only place

I could feel superior then,
watching the men in their leisure
suits and the funny shoes,
their fluffy-honey wives in toreadors

who always needed a few more
pointers just to get it wrong again.
I began to learn the strange
power that comes of watching well:

I knew the exhilaration in a mounting
score for Flo's Boutique or Genuine
Auto Parts. I wanted for myself
these simple feats destined

to be the life of the next beer-
blast. I began to want something
funny to tell the guys down
at some plant—

instead of only the wondering
at how things happen, at how
people I loved and people I didn't
crept up on me even while

I was paying attention,
at how I'd come to be sitting
night after night
between the soda fountain

and the scorers' benches,
unwelcome in the old
neighborhood
once more.

MARK COX

The Barbells of the Gods

It's a Thursday, getting late,
and we're the last three cars in the lot.
Richard has his face in his golf clubs
like they're flowers and smell nice,
and Buster is already talking bowling balls and shoes,
talking us slowly out of summer,
when Rich looks up sideways and says he's never been
with one man long enough to watch a pair of jeans fade
and what's it like being married to women?
Out on the lake there's that kind of silence that's loud—
two suns moving towards each other, one perfect, the other
just a glare—and I clean and jerk one last beer
and we talk about desire,
but nobody here, our legs dangling over fenders,
knows what he wants or how to get it any more
than when we were kids
and girls spent their adolescence as the hood ornament
of some boy's father's car. It's too
complicated, Buster says.
And he means the rule book is immense,
that there doesn't seem to be a clear point
or object to him.
But I say, You must have dreams of growing old
with one person
and how has it been so hard, pardon the pun,
no offense, to find the right guy? . . .
I did, Richard breaks in, but he's married,
so that's kind of why I'm asking you.
And I say, oh,
and Buster says, let's go someplace noisy
where we can really talk

ROBERT CRAWFORD

Downtown Sunday

The amputated husband
stumbles through downtown—
he reaches for a hand
that is no more his own.

The young widow's shadow
leans over the candle
in the shaded window
as if whispering farewell.

In morning's stubborn mist
the headlights push on:
Main Street's like a lost
funeral procession.

SILVIA CURBELO

Among Strangers

One lost track of the story.
One counted the black flowers on my dress
instead of sheep. One sold cars for a living.
One dreamed in three foreign languages
and never left the room.
One slept badly when he slept at all.
One imagined destiny
and desire were hopelessly
intertwined, but misguided, like lovers
who live in different cities and spend
all their Sundays together in bed.
One believed the isosceles triangle was a hoax.
One spoke only when spoken to.
One loved the light after a long rain.
One thought a broken wineglass
would make the perfect suicide note.
One married young. One never left.
One believed only geometry could steer
our displaced sensibilities.
One said a woman's sorrow was an aphrodisiac.
One lay down in the middle of the room
with the pale garments of the past
fanned all around him.
One never loved me.
One licked his empty plate.

KENNETH ZAMORA DAMACION

Canciones

What told us that the day was over?
The shadows that bled together over the tired earth?
The sun that dropped behind the mountains?
Remember, brother, how we followed
the pickers who sang mariachi music to one
another, egged each other with profanity
or a high yell that arched over the treetops
more piercing than the scorching sun?—
Remember how we sat beneath the eucalyptus,
our paychecks lost to beer from the Japanese market?
One season the names were Pedro, Ramon,
the next season they were different.
Did they remember the two boys they taught
to drink and sing each summer?
Each summer we hoped never to return.

Of what longings did the men sing?—
of women they left behind,
of complaints about the hard work
they had resigned themselves to.
Those summers when the straps from
the heavy canvas bags seemed to cut into our flesh
I wished that the orchards would vanish,
be paved over by blacktop and malls.
Now I wish I could renege on that curse.
Look where the houses are and the golf course;
these are the orchards where
we used to work, and beyond the mountains,

where the orange sun is setting, are the vineyards.
Brother, perhaps, there's one orchard left,
men sitting on crates and laughing in the dark.
Perhaps, they'll call out to us.

ROBERT DANA

The Mark

Shatterfall. Scutter
of leaf on asphalt
in a motel parking lot.
The Georgia morning,
blue slate; air,
edged. The man, there,
suddenly, beside your
rented car, saying,
"Now lissen 'a me.
Wait. I ain't gonna
do nuthin'. I ain't
gonna hurt you."
His eyes are bright.
He holds his hands
up, palms open.
They're small hands.
The hands of a man
who's never won
anything in his whole
life. "My name David,
an' I got these two
li'l babies at home.
They starvin'. They
need milk. Lissen 'a
me now. My woman sick,
an ah been to da
homeless shelter.
Tha's where I got this
jacket, see? It new,

see? 'Cause las' night
Halloween an' we had
a fire. It burn my
house an' my woman
she sick an' these
two li'l babies an'
lissen 'a me now,
I had go in there
an' get 'em. See?"
He extends his left
hand. He sees I see
no burn mark there.
"I'm gonna show ya
somethin' else, too.
Now, wait. I ain't
gonna hurt ya nor
nothin'. I jus' had
a kidney operation
las' year, unner-
stan'? See there?"
He lifts his t-shirt.
The scar is there.
A neat, twelve-inch,
chocolate welt curving
from back to belly.
"What do you need?"
I ask. (I'm a connoisseur
of scars.) "How much
do you need?" He takes
the proffered money,
nods, and goes. A look

in those bright eyes,
even now, in memory,
I cannot read.
Was his story true?
It doesn't matter.
Was I a sucker?
an easy mark? a soft
touch? The scar
was old, well-healed.
It doesn't matter.
This isn't literature.
This isn't about truth.

CHRISTOPHER DAVIS

The Murderer

As I talked, I kept thinking,
You're only guilty if they
can find it: but they'd fixed pads
to my temples and wrists. Now
I want to tell them something.
Last night, in a dream,
I watched a crusted gray whale
dying underwater, the bad end
of a steel harpoon
broken off in its side.
It was going down slowly,
horizontal, turning over
on its back, on its belly,
the blood weaving out
and wrapping around its whole length
like a frayed blanket. Then it
broke through a school of thousands
of tiny silver fish
and disappeared.
I guess it hit bottom. The blanket
kept unraveling up from the shadows,
staining all the water, all
the fish, and even filtered
weak columns of sunlight.
I woke, and lay half an hour
on my iron bed.
I hardly know what I've done.

DIANA DER-HOVANESSIAN

Exiles

My father, listening
to the broadcast news,
my mother said,
was exactly the same
as her father,
intent on every word
as if perhaps
he could lose
something added
since the last was heard.
The Monitor,
The New York Times consumed,
every hour on the hour
hushing the room,
they leaned toward news
that never came.

TOI DERRICOTTE

Passing

A professor invites me to his "Black Lit" class; they're
reading Larson's *Passing*. One of the black
students says, "Sometimes light-skinned blacks
think they can fool other blacks,
but *I* can always tell," looking
right through me.
After I tell them I am black,
I ask the class, "Was I passing
when I was just sitting here,
before I told you?" A white woman
shakes her head desperately, as if
I had deliberately deceived her.
She keeps examining my face,
then turning away
as if she hopes I'll disappear. Why presume
"passing" is based on what I leave out
and not what she fills in?
In one scene in the book, in a restaurant,
she's "passing,"
though no one checked her at the door—
"Hey, you black?"
My father, who looked white,
told this story: every year
when he'd go to get his driver's license,
the man at the window filling
out the form would ask,
"White or black?" pencil poised, without looking up.
My father wouldn't pass, but he might
use silence to trap a devil.

When he didn't speak, the man
would look up at my father's face.
"What do you think
he would always write?" my father'd say.

GREGORY DJANIKIAN

In the Elementary School Choir

I had never seen a cornfield in my life,
I had never been to Oklahoma,
But I was singing as loud as anyone,
"Oh what a beautiful morning. . . . The corn
Is as high as an elephant's eye,"
Though I knew something about elephants I thought,
Coming from the same continent as they did,
And they being more like camels than anything else.

And when we sang from *Meet Me in St. Louis*,
"Clang, clang, clang went the trolley,"
I remembered the ride from Ramleh Station
In the heart of Alexandria
All the way to Roushdy where my grandmother lived,
The autos on the roadway vying
With mule carts and bicycles,
The Mediterranean half a mile off on the left,
The air smelling sharply of diesel and salt.

It was a problem which had dogged me
For a few years, this confusion of places,
And when in 5th grade geography I had pronounced
"Des Moines" as though it were a village in France,
Mr. Kephart led me to the map on the front wall,
And so I'd know where I was,
Pressed my forehead squarely against Iowa.
Des Moines, he'd said. Rhymes with coins.

Now we were singing "zippidy-doo-dah, zippidy-ay,"
And every song we'd sung had in it
Either sun or bluebirds, fair weather

Or fancy fringe, O beautiful America!
And one tier below me,

There was Linda Deemer with her amber waves
And lovely fruited plains,
And she was part of America too
Along with sun and spacious sky
Though untouchable, and as distant
As purple mountains of majesty.

"This is my country," we sang,
And a few years ago there would have been
A scent of figs in the air, mangoes,
And someone playing the oud along a clear stream.

But now it was "My country 'tis of thee"
And I sang it out with all my heart
And now with Linda Deemer in mind.
"Land where my fathers died," I bellowed,
And it was not too hard to imagine
A host of my great-uncles and -grandfathers
Stunned from their graves in the Turkish interior
And finding themselves suddenly
On a rock among maize and poultry
And Squanto shaking their hands.

How could anyone not think America
Was exotic when it had Massachusetts
And the long tables of thanksgiving?
And how could it not be home
If it were the place where love first struck?

We had finished singing.
The sun was shining through large windows

On the beatified faces of all
Who had sung well and with feeling.

We were ready to file out and march back
To our room where Mr. Kephart was waiting.
Already Linda Deemer had disappeared
Into the high society of the hallway.
One day I was going to tell her something.
Des Moines, I was saying to myself,
Baton Rouge. Terre Haute. Boise.

STEPHEN DOBYNS

Exile

The time came for him to be released
from prison. Many years had passed
and, although he understood from TV
about the changes, he felt unprepared
for what he found. So when the prison

closed—it was very old—and the inmates
were sent to a new facility, he went back.
He called himself a caretaker, though no one
paid him, and he wore blue overalls—
not quite a prisoner, not quite a guard.

He wandered the yard where he had spent
so much time. He swept cells. He even
set up a small stove in the old kitchen.
He visited the deepest isolation cells,
places he had only heard about. Often

he was drawn to the room where executions
had been held. Though empty, the room felt
crowded with the many who had died there.
Meanwhile the world endured its variations.
Fashions changed, presidents were elected,

wars resumed, taxes were collected. At times
the man stared out from a barred window
at the city across the bay, admiring the tall,
glossy buildings, or he looked over the wall
at the graceful bridge and lines of traffic.

How manageable it seemed. And didn't this
comfort him and give him cheer when he went

back to a cell to finish some useless task—
plastering, painting, polishing—which, surely,
he didn't need to do? He worked even faster.

He felt passionate. What reasons must he have
given himself about why he did what he did.
The outside world had become a benign shadow.
As for what lay inside, he called it his life:
the unruly fiction which he labored to believe.

LYNN DOMINA

Pharaoh's Army Got Drownded

The cop's face for an odd second
looks as bloated as the face of a drowned
corpse, its puffy blue lips, its pallid skin.
Stumbling from the ticketed passengers' waiting room, he waves
his arms above his head and shouts
two names: *Sodom and Gomorrah,*
Sodom and Gomorrah, Sodom
and Gomorrah. I hate him instantly

and thoroughly. Then the paramedics
wheel a stretcher
from the men's room. The body
is wearing a yellow gauzy dress
and is bleeding from the mouth and is bruised
around the eyes. I watch
my skin achieve perfect stillness.
I watch my hand reach
toward him, my finger brushing away a trickle
of blood as a lover
would wipe away a tear.
Do you know this guy? another cop asks.
I try
to imagine his jaw without its swelling, his eyes
without their puffiness, his skin
without the blush. I try to remember
having seen him anywhere, and I try
to believe he has not been killed.
Still I fail
at recognition, and so I lie,
proclaiming my guilt as the guilty

will proclaim their innocence: *Yes,*
I tell the cop, *I know him.*

Early the next morning, I am walking
across a parking lot when I pause
before a rusted-out hatchback
with a police officer's decal in its rear window,
the bumper sticker announcing *God
Hates Faggots.* I am too exhausted
for fury, yet my left hand lifts the windshield wiper
to secure beneath it the note
my right hand has written: *May God
have mercy on your soul.*

The ambulance was swift
and I was not forced to admit
my false witness
until he was wheeled toward the morgue.
All night the cops
badgered me: *How could you
have made such a claim,* as if I should need
a reason past grief
in any world but ours.

MARK DOTY

Homo Will Not Inherit

Downtown anywhere and between the roil
of bathhouse steam—up there the linens of joy
and shame must be laundered again and again,

all night—downtown anywhere
and between the column of feathering steam
unknotting itself thirty feet above the avenue's

shimmered azaleas of gasoline,
between the steam and the ruin
of the Cinema Paree (marquee advertising

its own milky vacancy, broken showcases sealed,
ticketbooth a hostage wrapped in tape
and black plastic, captive in this zone

of blackfronted bars and bookstores
where there's nothing to read
but longing's repetitive texts,

where desire's unpoliced, or nearly so)
someone's posted a xeroxed headshot
of Jesus: permed, blonde, blurred at the edges

as though photographed through a greasy lens,
and inked beside him, in marker strokes:
HOMO WILL NOT INHERIT. *Repent & be saved.*

I'll tell you what I'll inherit: the margins
which have always been mine, downtown after hours
when there's nothing left to buy,

the dreaming shops turned in on themselves,
seamless, intent on the perfection of display,
the bodegas and offices lined up, impenetrable:

edges no one wants, no one's watching. Though
the borders of this shadow-zone (mirror and dream
of the shattered streets around it) are chartered

by the police, and they are required,
some nights, to redefine them. But not now, at twilight,
permission's descending hour, early winter darkness

pillared by smoldering plumes. The public city's
ledgered and locked, but the secret city's boundless;
from which do these tumbling towers arise?

I'll tell you what I'll inherit: steam,
and the blinding symmetry of some towering man,
fifteen minutes of forgetfulness incarnate.

I've seen flame flicker around the edges of the body,
pentecostal, evidence of inhabitation.
And I have been possessed of the god myself,

I have been the temporary apparition
salving another, I have been his visitation, I say it
without arrogance, I have been an angel

for minutes at a time, and I have for hours
believed—without judgement, without condemnation—
that in each body, however obscured or recast,

is the divine body—common, habitable—
the way in a field of sunflowers
you can see every bloom's

the multiple expression
of a single shining sea,
which is the face hammered into joy.

I'll tell you what I'll inherit:
stupidity, erasure, exile
inside the chalked lines of the police,

who must resemble what they punish,
the exile you require of me,
you who's posted this invitation

to a heaven nobody wants.
You who must be patrolled,
who adore constraint, I'll tell you

what I'll inherit, not your pallid temple
but a real palace, the anticipated
and actual memory, the moment flooded

by skin and the knowledge of it,
the gesture and its description
—do I need to say it?—

the flesh *and* the word. And I'll tell you,
you who can't wait to abandon your body,
what you want me to, maybe something

like you've imagined, a dirty story·
Years ago, in the baths,
a man walked into the steam,

the gorgeous deep indigo of him gleaming,
solid tight flanks, the intricately ridged abdomen—
and after he invited me to his room,

nudging his key toward me,
as if perhaps I spoke another tongue
and required the plainest of gestures,

after we'd been, you understand,
worshipping a while in his church,
he said to me, *I'm going to punish your mouth.*

I can't tell you what that did to me.
My shame was redeemed then;
I won't need to burn in the afterlife.

It wasn't that he hurt me,
more than that: the spirit's transactions
are enacted now, here—no one needs

your eternity. This failing city's
radiant as any we'll ever know,
paved with oily rainbow, charred gates

jeweled with tags, swoops of letters
over letters, indecipherable as anything
written by desire. I'm not ashamed

to love Babylon's scrawl. How could I be?
It's written on my face as much as on
these walls. This city's inescapable,

gorgeous, and on fire. I have my kingdom.

ELLEN DUDLEY

Pathologist

If he turns them, they are purple, black from head to heel,
every spot that hits the table livid with death,
the neat Y sliced on the torso, clean skin, bloodless muscle.

Now he wakes in the bloody light
of the City of Angels, his matutinal erection
snuffling the sheets. And as the alarm goes off,
he can't move, imagines his greater trochanter sinking
to the mattress, platform, all the way through the slab
of rented house to earth. It hurts
and he thinks the blood has gathered not in his penis where
he can feel every exquisite nerve but in the sleeping hip.
Though his lonely cock tells him he's alive, what he feels
at fifty is the hip, the shoulder, inert as a cadaver's.
And if he had a woman here in the angry morning light
he might pretend, forget for a minute his body.

He thinks: how beautiful the dead are,
those not disfigured by disease or gunshot, but say,
a suicide by pills. More radiant than the living,
that pewter sheen of skin. At rest. Perfect.
Just yesterday he placed his little fingers on a dead woman's
hipbones and stretched his hands, thumbs meeting on the navel.
Then stripping off his gloves he lay his hands full on her
cool belly, his whole body tingling.

VALERIE DUFF

Letters from an Exile

Trotsky's dead. My strays
crouch in bed. All night,
cup after cup from the samovar,
end of the revolution,
the cat tail's twitch. This
is how I melt the glacier,
chisel out the past. *Comrade,*
we thought we could set them all free.
If I were still welcome,
you'd be here. Marx was important,
rights were important.
If I were still welcome.

Comrade, old clothing
stuffed under the door,
I talk to myself about
world events. Rinse the face,
move lamp from desk to shelf to desk,
shorn neck, skullcap tied tight
to the bone. I'm gazing
at your photograph. *Comrade.* Why I write
is beyond me. Go to sleep. Extracting
ticks and brush from our hair, evenings
in the settlement, remember?
We painted and cooked,
walked barefoot, remember?
We argue, we sweat.

STEPHEN DUNN

The Guardian Angel

Afloat between lives and stale truths,
    he realizes
he's never truly protected one soul,

they all die anyway, and what good
    is solace,
solace is cheap. The signs are clear:

the drooping wings, the shameless thinking
    about utility
and self. It's time to stop.

The guardian angel lives for a month
    with other angels,
sings the angelic songs, is reminded

that he doesn't have a human choice.
    The angel of love
lies down with him, and loving

restores to him his pure heart.
    Yet how hard it is
to descend into sadness once more.

When the poor are evicted, he stands
    between them
and the bank, but the bank sees nothing

in its way. When the meek are overpowered
    he's there, the thin air
through which they fall. Without effect

he keeps getting in the way of insults.
    He keeps wrapping
his wings around those in the cold.

Even his lamentations are unheard,
    though now,
in for the long haul, trying to live

beyond despair, he believes, he needs
    to believe
everything he does takes root, hums

beneath the surfaces of the world.

EDISON DUPREE

At Present I Am Working as a Security Guard,

watching a mallard, just beyond
the far shore of the glistening
pesticide research pond.
He limps eccentrically along,

above his slung reflection.
It vibrates, and the colors flare
like a video malfunction.
I think he'd dive for the pond's floor,

and leave me tapping the guard-office
window with my keys,
if he were not of a surface-
feeding species.

LOUISE ERDRICH

The Lady in the Pink Mustang

The sun goes down for hours, taking more of her along
than the night leaves her with.
A body moving in the dust
must shed its heavy parts in order to go on.

Perhaps you have heard of her, the Lady in the Pink Mustang,
whose bare lap is floodlit from under the dash,
who cruises beneath the high snouts of semis, reading
the blink of their lights. *Yes. Move Over. Now.*
or *How Much.* Her price shrinks into the dark.

She can't keep much trash in a Mustang,
and that's what she likes. Travel light. Don't keep
what does not have immediate uses. The road thinks ahead.
It thinks for her, a streamer from Bismarck to Fargo
bending through Minnesota to accommodate the land.

She won't carry things she can't use anymore.
Just a suit, sets of underwear, what you would expect
in a Pink Mustang. Things she could leave anywhere.

There is a point in the distance where the road meets itself,
where coming and going must kiss into one.
She is always at that place, seen from behind,
motionless, torn forward, living in a zone
all her own. It is like she has burned right though time,
the brand, the mark, owning the woman who bears it.

She owns them, not one will admit what they cannot
come close to must own them. She takes them along,
traveling light. It is what she must face every time
she is touched. The body disposable as cups.

To live, instead of turn, on a dime.
One light point that is so down in value.
Painting her nipples silver for a show, she is thinking
You out there. What do you know.

Come out of the dark where you're safe. Kissing these
bits of change, stamped out, ground to a luster,
is to kiss yourself away piece by piece
until we're even. Until the last
coin is rubbed for luck and spent.
I don't sell for nothing less.

MARTÍN ESPADA

Beloved Spic

— *Valley Stream, Long Island 1973*

Here in the new white neighborhood,
the neighbors kept it pressed
inside dictionaries and Bibles
like a leaf, chewed it for digestion
after a heavy dinner,
laughed when it hopped
from their mouths like a secret,
whispered it as carefully as the answer
to a test question in school,
bellowed it in barrooms
when the alcohol
made them want to sing.

So I saw it
spraypainted on my locker and told no one,
found it scripted in the icing on a cake,
touched it stinging like the tooth slammed
into a faucet, so I kept my mouth closed,
pushed it away crusted on the coach's lip
with a spot of dried egg,
watched it spiral into the ear
of a disappointed girl who never sat beside me again,
heard it in my head when I punched a lamp,
mesmerized by the slash oozing
between my knuckles,
and it was beloved
until the day we staked our lawn
with a sign that read: For Sale.

ROGER FANNING

In the Barn

A cat composed as an uncut pie
sits on a rope-chafed rafter
and watches a boy, about fourteen, in overalls
apply mascara. What kind of future
can a boy like that have?
What useful work will he ever do?
He lies back on unbaled hay, his features lit
with a picture he saw in a magazine.
The cat blinks six times quick
seeing him come.
Then the cat climbs down
and licks his hand. Observer and introvert:
how they beg to be devoured.

MARTIN JUDE FARAWELL

Everything I Need to Know I Learned in Kindergarten

I sit
in the second-to-last seat
in the row
by the windows.
Teacher gives us each
a crayon,
a clean sheet
of construction paper,
says, we begin
with writing
our names.

The children
hunch over,
ignoring everything
but this naming.
I am the only one
no one's shown
my few pieces
of the alphabet.

She walks quietly
to my blank face,
blank paper.
Is kind.
Takes the crayon gently.
Asks my name. I am
the dumbest one in the room.

DONALD FINKEL

The Party

They're throwing a party upstairs.
He can hear it carom off the walls and fall
on his sweat-streaked ceiling.

Fretful as a splinter, he'd like
to join the party, senator
from the state of dislocation,
his infinitesimal pressure against history
faint as starlight thrumming the hairs
on a general's wrist.

He ascends from his coldwater grotto,
bobs through the flotsam, fetches up
on a stool by the anchovies.
A mermaid stoops to inquire: *What do*
you do? Her baubles dangle
in the weedy shadow.

I feed on air, he smiles,
like an orchid. I do
with, my delectable sea-grape.
I do without.

BRANDEL FRANCE DE BRAVO

Unrepentant

What could I do
when I saw his face
but send that baby back.
His eyes empty as a cob
without kernels.
His mouth like a hollow gourd,
cracked and dusty
as the midwife's hands.

One rainy season and one dry
I ate every day the flat bread
my husband's mother made for me.
I did not know,
coming from upriver,
anything of their customs.

If our sons ask to marry a girl
not of our tribe, it is true,
we tell them
drive the bride price down.
But once married the girls
never want for anything.
We feed them for the first year
from the crops of our forefathers.
We feed them the food of belonging
so that we may love them
as we do our own daughters.

As my mother-in-law talked
I saw for the first time

the cowrie shells she wears
are like a woman's sex with teeth.

When planting time came
I was so big
I had to open wide my knees
to bend and sow the seed.

One day my hoe hit rock
or what I thought was rock.
My husband's mother and sisters,
hearing the hitch in my breath,
came to where I was standing.
It was my first time to see
a head picked clean by death.
It is nothing, the sisters said.
It is our way, the mother said.

Beneath these fields are buried
the skulls of the great ancestors.
To you we gave bread made from flour
from the field where Molefi,
the healer, lies.
At first we used to hear him
whispering in the wheat,
words we could not understand.
Then he started knocking,
calling out, wanting to come in.
Through you we will know
his wisdom once again.

Behind the house
with only the gossip

of the roof's fronds
for company, I dug a hole
four hands deep
and lay the newborn down.
Then I pushed the piles
of dirt back in,
patting and flattening
until the ground was smooth
like a girl's stomach
before marriage.
Only then did his
keening cries quiet.

I say let the old medicine man
look for some other womb-door
though I may be punished
with no one to eat the grain grown
from my young bones.

CAROL FROST

Consent

Arrows striking all sides of the body and St. Sebastian smiling—
his torso, the shoulder that flinches inadvertently, through the neck
    hole of his robe.
Suddenly he seems to have forgotten thirst, hate, fear of perishing,—
    consented,—
and the bowmen put down their bows.
Thus it has been. All were silent, but it was in his silence that the next
    morning came.
And they who'd shot him against their will,
who'd eaten and slept with others in the night and been utterly alone,
hoped he'd be gone,—his torn body under the soil. When they had
    him tied to a tree,
what did they have? standing full of memory, feeling the feathers
    scythe through the air,
displacing the sounds, trusting his god's descriptions as he leaned his
    head to his—
a little of what already exists and the towering sense of kindnesses no
    world can offer?

FORREST GANDER

Deflection Toward the Relative Minor

for Jock O'Hazledean

They were partakers of a strange taste.   At the hour when
Everyone looks for   the passage to his own door
They went at large like   horses. His foot
Wore the steps to her porch.   They were often seen together
Under a dwarf chestnut.   It was said
She had fastened a pin in his walls.   It was said
He had given her his portion,   the firstfruits, and the
Trespass offering,   and the gift of shoulders. His spirit
Was greatly set on fire.

So with grum sentences,   we reproached the pair,
Declaring three similitudes,   showing them their error and
The moth. Explaining   how times wax
Old, they should   suffer straight things, draw in
The common air.

Secretly we prepared   a time to examine him
With despitefulness, to fill   all the places of her joy
With her torn hair.   With resin, pitch, and tow,
And small wood we stoked the oven.   But when we came
To arrest them   we were astonished.
Like the keel's trace   in the waves, they were not there.
They were gone together   over the wall into the wilderness
And no one of us followed   but wrote down their names
And buried the paper   in the evening ground when the bell
Sounded for prayer.

RICHARD GARCIA

Nobody Here but Us

Being old is not so bad. You wake up
from a nap and it's a new day in a new world,
at least that's what I say when I wake
to find myself in a rocking chair on the front porch
of the Swannanoa Convalescent Home.
What do I see when I look out at the sun
going flat in the haze of the Smoky Mountains?
I see chickens, thousands of them marching two by two
into the sizzling glow, as if into a frying pan.

Back in my carnival days, I used to hypnotize chickens.
I'd hold one close to my face and stare straight into its eyes,
and that chicken would freeze and plop over, stiff
as an old boot. Waving my arms, the cape, mumbo jumbo,
that was just showmanship. Who would pay to see a man
staring at a chicken? Obstinate. That's their whole problem.

Chickens are obstinate just like apes who could talk
if they wanted to—if they wanted to, chickens could fly.
I don't mean jump from a barn or into a tree but fly,
fill the sky, migrate, rise with the vultures on a warm
spiral staircase of air. You could put them in a wind tunnel,
maybe just a big, clear plastic tube with a fan at one end,
pull up and down on strings attached to their wings,
and play some stirring music like John Philip Sousa
or the theme from *Rocky,* and they'd still refuse to fly.

Dreams I had, words I might have said, something I read,
they get mixed up until I can't tell which was which.
Did I really catch Richard Nixon in my hen house?
And did he say he thought it was a voting booth? Was there
a gunfight? And did I leave town hanging from a rail,

tar and feathers my only clothing? I seem to remember
throwing an entire chicken dinner at the ceiling, my wife crying.

They used to love my act. I'd look down from the back of a truck
at all the blank-faced, crossed-eyed, beak-nosed farmers,
a drum would roll and I'd put that chicken's entire head
into my mouth and bite it off. The crowd would scream.
I'd spit the head into some lady's lap—flap my elbows,
knock my knees together, strut, crow, cock-a-doodle-do,
and spin that chicken over my head, spraying blood like rain.

ETHAN GILSDORF

The Walk

Why must that slight man
pause,
　　　that man I pass
each day with coffee on Main Street,
　　　　　pausing after each
accurate step,

adjusting his State Farm hat scarlet
as the tributaries
　　　　mapped along his nose,
checking the rented pay phones
for change
　　　I hope he doesn't need.

He avoids each anxious crack.
　　　He can't dismiss his mother's back.
To walk would be to continue,
to find a new plane to rest his eyes,
　　　to not shoot the old mutt behind the shed,
　　　　　to find something in the salvage pile
of tangled forgets and wants,
maybe an old eagerness for spring.
　　　　　　　With each rest he immobilizes
　　　　his life and draws it into mine.

He doesn't care.
　　　Anvils of clouds are edged with pink, and
he doesn't care what I might think
and walks on,
　　　　with precision,

as if each step was the sum
of everything he's learned. He walks,

stops,

walks. His body is unprepared
                    for neon. He draws his jacket tight.
I worry he will soon choose Spandex
over drab green Dickies and a baseball cap.

    For now, in each hand a thin plastic bag
swings heavy with salami and beer.
                                        I'm ready to stop.
But he crosses the vacant common,
past the library's home for obsolescence,
            past the unrealized storefronts.
He may need to live.
                    I worry
this is no world for old men.

MICHAEL S. GLASER

Magnificat!

Tonight, on holiday in Oxford, Bach's *Magnificat*.
The top windows of the Sheldonian are open and music
surrounds the building, drifting down Broad Street
where we walk in the cool of evening's extended light.

Eva races down the cobbled path, leaps small tour jetés
on the gravel. We try to hush her exuberance,
but her grin is too full, the brightness
in her eyes too light, too light . . .

Watching her, I think of my grandfather telling how
in the old country, near Kiev, his family locked
their doors and hid in the basement each Easter
when the Christians, leaving church, raced down
the cobbled streets of the Jews, hurling stones
and dung at anyone they saw, chanting
"Christ killer, Christ killer . . ."

This evening, the inheritance of generations overwhelms:
the impossibility of even imagining all this,
years ago when grandfather, escaping from Russia,
knocked down a guard and ran for his life, for the life
of this very child, running with abandon,
to the sounds of the *Magnificat*—

Gloria Patri, Gloria Filio,
Gloria et spiritui sancto.

MICHELE GLAZER

Star-Spangled

One man won't say anything.

One says over to himself
        oh say can you see

anything

The world rolls under his tongue
as a muddy river enjoins the bank

join me. Or
            watch me

        roll on.

Fourteen years later and he's still fresh home from Nam.

If he could just tell his story he'd get

a better job. More money. His health back.
If he had time

doing it would be as easy as two sticks.

Afraid of missing
                something

he leans forward—
        What is the difference between a subject
        and a noun Why do we need both Do
        rhetorical questions get question
        marks Why
                do we need both

How does it feel to be back

I want to ask him and

How does it feel to be you

His secret is he knows
he doesn't belong here.

One night I bring a cut-out, white
on black or black

on white, is the question.
Is it a vase or two faces seen

in profile and from a long distance?
Did "the tailback who injured his knee recently

return to practice"?
Or did he recently return?

That night the weather turns.
All night everything will happen

under one color.
In the middle of class he gets up,

walks out into it.
"Apostrophes show possession,"

says one woman after he leaves.
"But if you just say it

you don't need them."
One night in the middle of his question

he stops. His words
turn back to him suddenly, a black

funneling of swifts down a chimney.
It is a mystery why

they choose one chimney over another
and how so many birds fit inside.

LYLE GLAZIER

On TV
the face of the slaughtered
Cambodian child
is pure and innocent
as if she were resting
in her father's arms
yet the distant viewers
suppliers of weapons
do not cradle
the supple frail body
or kiss the petulant mouth,
they are like the Old Testament
Jehovah who took the firstborn
of Egypt for his fee,
but unlike the Hebrews
who as beneficiaries
were bereaved in sharing
the common doom of mankind,
the American watchers
see the young face fade from their channel
and do not mind going to dinner
hungry, in fact, as hell

ALBERT GOLDBARTH

The Book of Human Anomalies

Maud Stevens received her first tattoo in 1904,
when she met The Tattooed Globetrotter ("one of the last
tattooists to work by hand"), Gus Wagner, at the St. Louis World's
    Fair.
By 1912, when this photograph is taken, Mrs. Maud Stevens Wagner
is decorated as intricately, as heraldically, by Gus
as the Unicorn Tapestries at The Cloisters.

Ta-daa! Zacchini, the Human Projectile—caught here
flying at the apogee of his travel from the mouth
of the "Monster Repeating Cannon." The puff of smoke
is still visible, and Zacchini's arc is so high, he's
half out of the picture—as if, for a moment in 1930,
his razzle-dazzle science
has outdistanced the reach of photography.

In Pueblo, Colorado, on the fourth of July,
a Mrs. Eunice Padfield dived from a twenty-five-foot platform
to a waiting pool of water—on horseback.
Alexander Patty is shown performing his feat in which
he went up twelve stairs—bouncing all the way
on his head. The caption, mysteriously enough, says
he'd go "nine stairs down," but doesn't account
for the missing three. Like many of these performers
he's in formal attire and seems completely unruffled.

How much joy was there in this? How much
defiance? Somebody wearing a "suit" of live bees.
Somebody training the circus's elephant: *one foot,
up on one foot!*, all day, long days,
elephant smell and elephant food. Also the circus

accountant—his own applaudable
balancing act. The venues we choose. *Are* we
our venues? Someone, all day, certifying accountants.
Someone helping the elephant push out a twisted, difficult birth.

Mr. Cheerful Gardner ("The Human Pendulum")
trained elephants to lift him in their mouths,
by his head, and sway him back and forth.
Here's plucky sixteen-year-old Eleanor Link,
the alligator wrestler. Maria Speltering (1876) is daintily crossing
Niagara Falls on a tightrope, feet in bushel baskets.
A long day, a very long day.

And where its odd skin ends, the skin of the very long night
begins. She's in their bunting-covered and gargoyled touring wagon,
totaling up the evening's scant receipts—Maud Stevens Wagner—
when he steps inside, behind her (he's been out to tent
mosquito netting around the child's gargoyled crib),
and leisurely undoes her thick chignon. She
steps from her bone button dress . . . and then
by fingertip, and then by tongue, they trace the living pictures
they've stippled onto one another's flesh.
The child, making its snuffle noises . . .
The shuffled-up pile of bills on the table . . .
The lust-sound, and the argument-sound,
and the rhythms of the together-sound, and the simple
in and out of breath through our complex sleeps . . .
Astonishing.

note: for much of this information I rely on Mark Sloan's
Hoaxes, Humbugs and Spectacles

ALVIN GREENBERG

the man in the moon

white-faced, white-suited, as big as the full moon in the tropical sky
i've just dropped out of and as wheezy and confident as sidney
    greenstreet
in *the maltese falcon*, the fat man rolls my way across the waiting room

of the small airport in south india. it is 1966. in a sky of black faces
i have never seen anything whiter than this. it is the moon, the moon
in its tropical cotton and straw, wavering my way in some erratic
    orbit,

white jacket flapping, and i feel myself being drawn up into its lunatic
gravity. see how it parts the dark heavens between us! how even at
    dawn
it beams with the pleasure of its fullness! how to the stranger i am it

announces itself in its own reflected glare, with moony arms spread
    wide
and moony paw and cratered moony grin, as the head jew of cochin.

———

it's the being known i always battle. what was i wearing, a yellow star?
'bruder!' 'landsman!' how do they always know you, wherever you
    are?

up all night on the long flight east, i hardly knew myself for what i
    was.
was i this white? as small as me but beautiful and black the indian
    men
and women swirled like spiral galaxies in corners of the waiting
    room,

rippling from his passage, the pale, disturbing perturbations of the
    moon.

this is the way the cosmos curves, i guess, space in its curious
    symmetries
bending around some lump of the familiar, small objects caught and
    bound

by forces they neither like nor understand. i took a few steps back, but
our orbits were fixed by then. for a year we circled each other. he was
a decent, generous man, a sometimes host and help, never quite a
    friend.

        —

a quarter century old now, too white to say it fades, the memory . . .
wanes. occasionally, though, on clear summer nights when the full
    moon
washes most of the stars from the sky and there's an almost tropical
    smell

to even these northern woods, when the birch and balsam and pine
    exhale
their own exotic perfumes—and i was a stranger here, too, 25 years
    ago—
i remember that huge, pale, round-faced, white-suited man in the
    moon

looming suddenly over me, arms spread wide, trying to gather me up in
his ancient tidal surge. did i travel halfway around the world for that?
the stranger i was was the stranger i wanted to be. leave me alone,

i wanted to cry, even as I shook his hand. around us the dark, bright
faces sparkled. why was he even there? fact: it was his world, too:
there'd been jews in cochin for a thousand years. but he hung, in my

black sky like a terrible white sign: they know you wherever you are.

JOHN HAINES

On a Certain Field in Auvers

> There is something in my heart...
>   —Van Gogh

I

On the road to Hallucination,
pass by the yellow house
that is the house of friendship,
but is also the color of madness...

Stand by the roadside, braced
in the punishing wind that blows
on that field and another...
In the red dust of evening,
ask yourself these questions:

'Who made the sun, strenuous
and burning?'
                It was I.

'And the cypress, a green torrent
in the nightwind?'
                It was I.

'And the clock of evening, coiled
like a spring? ... Who turned
the stars in their sockets
and set them to spinning?'
                            It was I.

On the road to the Night Cafe,
where the light from a door

that is always open
spills over cobbles and tables;

where the pipesmoker calmed
his fury, a yellow chair
in which no one is sitting . . .

It is no one. It is I.

II
I, who never for one hour
forgot how the light seizes
both field and striding sower;
who held my hand steady
in the solar flame, and drank
for my thirst the fiery
mineral spirit of the earth.

Who remembered always, even
in the blistering south,
a cellar in the north
where a handful of stunted
people peeled their substance
day by day, and all their
dumb and patient misery
steeped in a cold green light.

On the road to the hospital
built of the great stones
of sorrow, and furnished
with chains and pillows . . .
In the red dust of evening
the Angelus is ringing.

And out among the haystacks,
strange at this late hour,
 a light, both moving and still,
 as if someone there was
 turning, a ring of candles
 burning in his hatbrim . . .

It is . . . no one.

        III
In the Asylum of Saint-Rémy,
that is also the burnt field
of Auvers; at the graveside
of two distracted brothers.

On this one day in July
we speak the rites for all
torn and departed souls.

And we hope that with
a hundred years of practice
we have learned to speak
the appropriate words:

'In the country of the deaf
a one-eared man was king . . .

'In the name of the poor,
and of the holy insane,
and the great light of the sun.'

FORREST HAMER

Line up

Once again, someone took me
for another black man, my brother
and someone else's, who robbed a store
or took a woman's precious,
stole back something lost to him. Someone
came up to me, slapped me in my face,
and made me prove I was not criminal
or minded of crime: told me
open up my coat and produce
that bottle of gin,
                    that driver's license,

                                that penis
they swore they saw me put there
as I'd gone about my business
                                presuming it belonged to me.

JOY HARJO

Anchorage

for Audre Lorde

This city is made of stone, of blood, and fish.
There are Chugatch Mountains to the east
and whale and seal to the west.
It hasn't always been this way, because glaciers
who are ice ghosts create oceans, carve earth
and shape this city here, by the sound.
They swim backwards in time.

Once a storm of boiling earth cracked open
the streets, threw open the town.
It's quiet now, but underneath the concrete
is the cooking earth,
                         and above that, air
which is another ocean, where spirits we can't see
are dancing   joking   getting full
on roasted caribou, and the praying
goes on, extends out.

Nora and I go walking down 4th Avenue
and know it is all happening.
On a park bench we see someone's Athabascan
grandmother, folded up, smelling like 200 years
of blood and piss, her eyes closed against some
unimagined darkness, where she is buried in an ache
in which nothing makes
                        sense.

We keep on breathing, walking, but softer now,
the clouds whirling in the air above us.

What can we say that would make us understand
better than we do already?
Except to speak of her home and claim her
as our own history, and know that our dreams
don't end here, two blocks away from the ocean
where our hearts still batter away at the muddy shore.

And I think of the 6th Avenue jail, of mostly Native
and Black men, where Henry told about being shot at
eight times outside a liquor store in L.A., but when
the car sped away he was surprised he was alive,
no bullet holes, man, and eight cartridges strewn
on the sidewalk
                    all around him.

Everyone laughed at the impossibility of it,
but also the truth. Because who would believe
the fantastic and terrible story of all of our survival,
those who were never meant
                         to survive?

JAMES HAUG

The Tennessee Waltz

He bows because he is nobody,
corrects the street
under its tilted little caps
of lamplight, and sets off again.
He sleeps near the railyards
where all night
the police come down
and trouble the stars,
club the soles of his feet,
move on, move on,
where the big engines bear down
at dawn
and rock the earth.
Too goddamn early, he swears,
when the hammers of morning
open a door in the sky.

At the Red Cross, they won't buy
blood like his. And why not
he wants to know,
the pint of Night Train
tucked in his back pocket,
and turns to the others waiting
in that room, his face
flushed dark as a bruise.
Night Train, he claims,
makes the blood red, see,
and under his thumb
bulges the thick green cords
of veins in his wrist.

But the nurse at her station
behind the sliding glass
won't have it, and tells him,
Come back when you're dry.

He turns and opens his arms,
cracks a stained grin
and enfolds the imaginary
body of a woman
in his careful, mute waltz.
The pint nearly empty,
he slumps into a folding chair
and rehearses the look of the world,
sober and meaningful
and quietly disengaged
from himself,
until he almost has it right,
the look of a man who waits
for a train
that will awaken the whole world.

ANITA HELLE

Poem for Natalia Ginzburg

When Natalia Ginzburg died, the papers of her region declared
    *The age of ideology has ended.** They buried her body
in two parts: In one coffin the half of her that was Catholic set off
    against the blue velvet ribbon of a necklace belonging to her
grandmother, and a ring of tiny flowers the women of Abruzzo carry on
    psalm days to the cemetery. In the other coffin they buried a rebel,
a communist Jew, and bound the remaining arm in a red tourniquet.
    The bier was strewn with pamphlets, along with the ashes, and a pair
of sunglasses she had worn the day the Italian resistance forces landed
    on the beach, their guns filled with sand and dirt. When
Natalie Ginzburg came around for a second life, the talk surrounding
    her grew equally misleading. Long before she took up residence
in the large Roman apartment and resumed the duties appropriate
    to a woman of her station, it was revealed she had been working
on a different language. It was one she couldn't speak, something
    between
    the structured intonations of a dialect and the inarticulate
slush of inner speech. Some compared it to a seething, such as
    can be heard when the sea drives and pitches against the low
rocks. Others heard in the rushing and breathing a deeper quiet,
    the nocturnal pause between two pronouns, *you* and *I.*

* "The age of ideology . . . has ended" is quoted from an essay, "Anchoring Natalia Ginzburg," by Wallis Wilde-Menozzi, *The Kenyon Review* 16 (1994) p. 116. I am grateful to Wilde-Menozzi for research and translation.

116

EMILY HIESTAND

The Day Lily and the Fox

An Irish soul walks away from Paddy's
late, and the shine on his cap comes
from a long pink neon tube for beer.

He's not drunk, you can see that,
but he misses all the cracks on the walk.
He'll be going home to his mother,

whose back he has not broken,
and to an oilcloth-covered table: flowers,
roosters, and yellow checks in the pattern.

When it's warm again he'll be stopping
at Saint Peter's field to see the players
pitch the A-league games at night.

He'll stay by the low fence with the boys
or squeeze, with a sno-cone, into the bleachers.
Paddy's will cream the Harvard Trust Bombers.

The notion is: the simple do less harm.
Do ye no harm sounds weak until you try,
and find each gesture harms—that a bowl

of cereal leaches the Iowa topsoil away.
Too much or too little adds to the heap
burning on the rubbish islands,

insulated from every soothing rain
(as little harm as the day lily or the fox).
The notion is: the meek will inherit,

that ones who watch daylong as jays
twine a nest are pure and holy spirits.
It wouldn't figure that the creative one

would elect the vacant and the sorry,
unless these come into the world to prove
our love—which itself would pull no weight

among the orbits, however popular,
unless it be a striking thing, adaptive
as gills, tendrils, fur or gripping tails.

EDWARD HIRSCH

Song

This is a song for the speechless,
the dumb, the mute and the motley,
the unmourned! This is a song for every
pig that was too thin to be slaughtered
last night, but was slaughtered
anyway, every worm that was hooked
on a hook that it didn't expect,
every chair in New York City that has
no arms or legs, and can't speak English,
every sofa that has ever been torn
apart by the children or the dog
and earmarked for the dump, every sheet
that was lost in the laundry, every
car that has been stripped down and
abandoned, too poor to be towed away,
too weak and humble to protest.
Listen, this song is for you even if
you can't listen to it, or join in;
even if you don't have lungs, even
if you don't know what a song is,
or want to know. This song is for
everyone who is not listening tonight
and refuses to sing. Not singing
is also an act of devotion; those
who have no voices have one tongue.

JONATHAN HOLDEN

Saturday Afternoon, October

Pure sunlight is strewn all over the lawn
like loose change through the sycamore leaves.
This town is as still as Sunday morning.
Over at Faurot Field, the game has begun.

Fat, unruly grackles are haggling for seats
in the upper sections of the walnut tree.
They all change seats at once in a dither
while keeping their eye on the big game above—
the slow move of the weather.

High in the crowd, squirrels are rummaging,
scolding all the players, even the spectators,
and hawking fat green walnuts.

I'm out of the game,
down here. My allegiance is with
this light, which doesn't care who wins.

I'm on nobody's team.

JANET HOLMES

Depressive Episode

It's funny, but I don't remember much.
By day a rhombus travels over walls
reputed to be white: when evening falls
the lot's halogen streetlight makes the switch
and keeps the pattern of that window etched
just opposite my bed. I want to sleep.
They give me drugs that promise some escape
but fail. I have a buzzing they can't touch.
I have a clarity that I can't reach.
Words will not come. The nurses will not talk
or care for me. The doctor tells me, later,
that this, regrettably, is normal. Such
is their perspective: Someone with the luck
of health has tried to take her life. They hate her.

REMY HOLZER

Current "Now, Voyager" Fantasy

I am standing tensely at the desk
and Claude Rains is examining my poems.

"Did you make these yourself?" he inquires,
a reddish lock of hair falling over his brow.

He comments on the skill. I tell him
I get the ivory from overseas, special.

I think he understands.
He says it's a matter of the doing.

Well, I keep looking at my razor, at any
bottle of pills, thinking, it's only a matter

Of the doing. I know what that is.
I want to see myself in black and white.

I'll step into the movie. I want to see
the last inch of my all-too-real flesh-colored

Heel melt into graded grays,
mercury and rainwater.

I want the big angled hat,
the best deck chair, the lit cigarette

Moist from Paul Henreid's lips.
I want to be there, elegant and effortless,

Slim and careful, the most "interesting"
passenger on board, the only real

Escapist, the aunt-no-longer Bostonian,
the Woman with a Past, the Voyager, Camille.

PAUL JENKINS

Six Small Fires

They hurry through the forest suitcases in hand
Bulging suitcases and young children
Pursued a half mile behind by brooms
Industrial-strength brooms or whatever you imagine
Gaining at the rate of two broom handles per song
The border I'm guessing thirty miles to go
Like a word-problem in math mixed oak and hemlock

You can tell by their faces they're not buying the brooms
The singing I invented because someone has to
You can tell by the light it's late afternoon
Like makeup smeared on the left halves of treetrunks
And by the dusk rising upward from their shoes
In the distance six small fires
In a clearing in a neat ring

It's like the presentation-dream every analyst loves
So the talking-cure has a crux to aim at
Doctor I can't clear the image from my brain
Except it's not dreaming I swear it's from life
In Grodno Forest dated 1940
All except for the six small fires
I set just now to witness my shame

DENIS JOHNSON

Poem

There was something I can't bring myself
to mention in the way the light
seemed trapped by the clouds,
the way the road dropped
from pavement to dirt and the land from pine
to scrub—
the red-headed vultures on dead animals,
the hatred of the waitress breaking

a cup and kicking the shards across the café
that looked out on the mountain and on the white smear
of the copper mine that sustained these people.
I claim there was something you wouldn't
have wanted to speak of either,
a sense of some violent treasure
like uranium waiting to be romanced
out of the land . . .

They sat under white umbrellas,
two or three together, elbows on card tables
at the dirt roads leading to the mines,
rising each at his turn to walk
around a while with a sign
announcing they were on strike,
their crystalline and indelible
faces in the hundred-degree
heat like the faces of slaughtered hogs,
and God forgive me,
I pulled to the side of the road and wrote this poem.

ALLISON JOSEPH

On Being Told I Don't Speak Like a Black Person

Emphasize the "h," you ignorant ass,
was what my mother was told
when colonial-minded teachers
slapped her open palm with a ruler
in that Jamaican schoolroom.
Trained in England, they tried
to force their pupils to speak
like Eliza Doolittle after
her transformation, fancying themselves
British as Henry Higgins,
despite dark, sun-ripened skin.
Mother never lost her accent,
though, the music of her voice
charming everyone, an infectious lilt
I can imitate, not duplicate.
No one in the States told her
to eliminate the accent,
my high school friends adoring
the way her voice would lift
when she called me to the phone:
A-lli-son, it's friend Cathy.
Why don't you sound like her?,
they'd ask. I didn't sound
like anyone or anything,
no grating New Yorker nasality,
no fastidious British mannerisms
like the ones my father affected
when he wanted to sell someone
something. And I didn't sound

like a Black American,
college acquaintances observed,
sure they knew what a black person
was supposed to sound like.
Was I supposed to sound lazy,
dropping syllables here, there,
not finishing words but
slurring final letters so that
each sentence joined the next,
sliding past the listener?
Were certain words off limits,
too erudite, too scholarly
for someone with a natural tan?
I asked what they meant,
and they stuttered, blushed,
said *you know, Black English*,
applying what they'd learned
from that semester's text.
Does everyone in your family
speak alike? I'd question,
and they'd say *don't take this*
the wrong way, nothing personal.
Now I realize there's nothing
more personal than speech,
that I don't have to defend
how I speak, how any person,
black, white, chooses to speak.
Let us speak. Let us talk
with the sounds of our mothers
and fathers still reverberating
in our minds, wherever our mothers

or fathers come from:
Arkansas, Belize, Alabama,
Brazil, Aruba, Arizona.
Let us simply speak
to one another,
listen and prize the inflections,
differences, never assuming
how any person will sound
until her mouth opens,
until his mouth opens,
greetings familiar
in any language.

LAWRENCE JOSEPH

Sand Nigger

In the house in Detroit
in a room of shadows
when grandma reads her Arabic newspaper
it is difficult for me to follow her
word by word from right to left
and I do not understand
why she smiles about the Jews
who won't do business in Beirut
"because the Lebanese
are more Jew than Jew,"
or whether to believe her
that if I pray
to the holy card of Our Lady of Lebanon
I will share the miracle.
Lebanon is everywhere
in the house: in the kitchen
of steaming pots, leg of lamb
in the oven, plates of kousa,
hushwee rolled in cabbage,
dishes of olives, tomatoes, onions,
roasted chicken, and sweets;
at the card table in the sunroom
where grandpa teaches me
to wish the dice across the backgammon board
to the number I want;
Lebanon of mountains and sea,
of pine and almond trees,
of cedars in the service
of Solomon, Lebanon
of Babylonians, Phoenicians, Arabs, Turks

and Byzantines, of the one-eyed
monk, Saint Maron,
in whose rite I am baptized;
Lebanon of my mother
warning my father not to let
the children hear,
of my brother who hears
and from whose silence
I know there is something
I will never know; Lebanon
of grandpa giving me my first coin
secretly, secretly
holding my face in his hands,
kissing me and promising me
the whole world.
My father's vocal cords bleed;
he shouts too much
at his brother, his partner,
in the grocery store that fails.
I hide money in my drawer, I have
the talent to make myself heard.
I am admonished to learn,
never to dirty my hands
with sawdust and meat.
At dinner, a cousin
describes his niece's head
severed with bullets, in Beirut,
in civil war. "More than
an eye for an eye," he demands,
breaks down, and cries.
My uncle tells me to recognize
my duty, to use my mind,

to bargain, to succeed.
He turns the diamond ring
on his finger, asks if
I know what asbestosis is,
"the lungs become like this,"
he says, holding up a fist;
he is proud to practice
law which "distributes
money to compensate flesh."
Outside the house my practice
is not to respond to remarks
about my nose or the color of my skin.
"Sand nigger," I'm called,
and the name fits: I am
the light-skinned nigger
with black eyes and the look
difficult to figure—a look
of indifference, a look to kill—
a Levantine nigger
in the city on the strait
between the great lakes Erie and St. Clair
which has a reputation
for violence, an enthusiastically
bad-tempered sand nigger
who waves his hands, nice enough
to pass, Lebanese enough
to be against his brother,
with his brother against his cousin,
with cousin and brother
against the stranger.

X. J. KENNEDY

Poets

These people are . . . quenched. I mean the natives.
—D. H. Lawrence,
letter from Dover, New Jersey

Le vierge, le vivace, et le bel aujourd'hui . . .

  What were they like as schoolboys? Long on themes
And short of wind, perpetually outclassed,
Breaking their glasses, always chosen last
  When everyone was sorted out in teams,

  Moody, a little dull, the kind that squirmed
At hurt cats, shrank from touching cracked-up birds,
With all but plain girls at a loss for words,
  Having to ask to have their fishhooks wormed,

  Snuffers of candles every priest thought nice,
Quenchers of their own wicks, their eyes turned down
And smoldering. In Dover, my home town,
  No winter passed but we had swans in ice,

  Birds of their quill: so beautiful, so dumb,
They'd let a window glaze about their feet,
Not seeing through their dreams till time to eat.
  A fireman with a blowtorch had to come

  Thaw the dopes loose. Sun-silvered, plumes aflap,
Weren't they grand, though? Not that you'd notice it,
Crawling along a ladder, getting bit,
  Numb to the bone, enduring all their crap.

ROD KESSLER

The Elm Tree on Lafayette Street

Thinks it's all junk these days, the routine,
insistent parade of Toyotas and Broncos
heading up to the college, the kid in the pickup
getting out the freebie Sunday paper every Saturday
around ten, the ladies boarding the 455 bus, two quarters
and a dime in hand, handbags full of certainties.
The Latin guys without jobs spend their mornings
on benches across from the donut shop and the Catholic
Church. In the frame shop, the artist who could do better
work with her eyes closed takes her time mounting yet
another print of Monet's garden from the museum shop
in the city. At Major MagLeashe's, the proprietor
squinting at daylight shows the door to the smells
of yesterday's beer spills. This is all junk, thinks
the great elm on Lafayette Street. It was junk
forty years ago too, for that matter, when little boys
wore ties every Monday for assembly at the Middle School,
the girls blue dresses, even though they didn't want to,
and all the mommies stayed home and had private breakdowns
and cooked chicken à la king. It is junk
and was junk, thinks the elm, whose every heavy limb turns
upward in its own sweet, unrepeated & rococo way. Limbs?
Branches? Only in the most literal sense *wooden*,
thinks the elm. The tree thinks its trunk and branches
are a jazz statement, as though jazz could be something
other than sound. Well, why the hell not, this elm tree
thinks. *Just look at me.* And it bugs him that we don't get it.

MAXINE HONG KINGSTON

Restaurant

for Lilah Kan

The main cook lies sick on a banquette, and his assistant
has cut his thumb. So the quiche cook takes
their places at the eight-burner range, and you and I
get to roll out twenty-three rounds of pie
dough and break a hundred eggs, four at a crack,
and sift out shell with a China cap, pack
spinach in the steel sink, squish and squeeze
the water out, and grate a full moon of cheese.
Pam, the pastry chef, who is baking Choco-
late Globs (once called Mulattos) complains about the disco,
which Lewis, the salad man, turns up louder out of spite.
"Black so-called musician." "Broads. Whites."
The porters, who speak French, from the Ivory Coast,
sweep up droppings and wash the pans without soap.
We won't be out of here until three A.M. In this basement,
I lose my size. I am a bent-over
child, Gretel or Jill, and I can
lift a pot as big as a tub with both hands.
Using a pitchfork, you stoke the broccoli and bacon.
Then I find you in the freezer, taking
a nibble of a slab of chocolate big as a table.
We put the quiches in the oven, then we are able
to stick our heads up out of the sidewalk into the night
and wonder at the clean diners behind glass in candlelight.

GALWAY KINNELL

Memory of Wilmington

Thirty-some years ago, hitchhiking
north on Route 1, I stopped for the night
at Wilmington, Delaware, one of those American cities
that start falling apart before they ever get finished.
I met, I remember, an ancient hobo—I almost remember
his name—at the ferry—now dead,
of course, him,
and also the ferry—
in great-brimmed hat, coat to his knees,
pants dragging the ground, semi-zootish rig
plucked off various clotheslines. I remember

he taught me how to grab a hen
so the dogs won't hear: how to come up on it
from behind, swoop down and swing it up
and whirl it, all in one motion,
breaking the neck, of course, also twisting
silent any cry
for help it might want to utter—

"give," I suppose, would be the idiom.

It doesn't matter.
It doesn't matter
that we ill-roasted our hen over brushwood
or that with the squeamishness
of the young I dismouthed the rawest of it
the fire hadn't so much as warmed and tossed it
behind me into the black waters of Delaware Bay.

After he ate, I remember, the old hobo
—*Amos!* yes, that was his name!—old Amos sang,

or rather laughed forth a song or two, his voice
creaking out slower and slower,
like the music in old music boxes, when time slows itself down in them.
I sat in the last light and listened, there among rocks,
tin cans, feathers, ashes, old stars. This. This.

The next morning the sun was out
when I sailed north on the ferry.
From the rotting landing Amos waved.
I was fifteen, I think. Wilmington then
was far along on its way to becoming a city
and already well advanced on its way back to dust.

CAROLYN KIZER

To an Unknown Poet

I haven't the heart to say
you are not welcome here.
Your clothes smell of poverty, illness
and unswept closets.
You come unannounced to my door
with your wild-faced wife and your many children.
I tell you I am busy.
I have a dentist's appointment.
I have a terrible cold.
The children would run mad
through our living room, with its collected
bibelots and objects of art.
I'm not as young as I was.
I am terrified of breakage.

It's not that I won't help you.
I'd love to send you a box
of hand-milled soap;
perhaps a check,
though it won't be enough to help.
Keep in mind that I came to your reading:
Three of us in the audience,
your wife, myself, and the bookstore owner,
unless we count the children who played trains
over your wife's knees in their torn jeans
and had to be hushed and hushed.

Next month I am getting an award
from the American Academy
and Institute of Arts and Letters.

The invitation came on hand-laid paper
thick as clotted cream.
I will travel by taxi
to 156th Street, where the noble old building,
as pale as the Acropolis,
is awash in a sea of slums.
And you will be far away, on the other coast,
as far from our thoughts as Rimbaud
with his boy's face and broken teeth,
while we eat and drink and congratulate each other
in this bastion of culture.

BILL KNOTT

Christmas at the Orphanage

But if they'd give us toys and twice the stuff
most parents splurge on the average kid,
orphans, I submit, need more than enough;
in fact, stacks wrapped with our names nearly hid
the tree: these sparkling allotments yearly
guaranteed a lack of—what?—family?—

I knew exactly what it was I missed
as we were lined up number rank and file:
to share my pals' tearing open their piles
meant sealing the self, the child that wanted
to scream at all *You stole those gifts from me;*
whose birthday is worth such words? The wish-lists
they'd made us write out in May lay granted
against starred branches. I said I'm sorry.

RON KOERTGE

Lazarus

After Jesus raised him from the dead
and everyone was impressed, He went on
His way while Lazarus stayed home with Mary
and Martha, who put together a nice little party,
just family and friends, but nice, with plenty
of wine and colored lanterns in the trees.

"Don't shake hands," advised one guest,
"he's colder than a well-digger's ass."
"Lazarus is pale as hell," whispered Uncle Enoch.
A niece added, "Lazarus stinks."

Pretty soon they had him sitting nine yards
away from the table, wrapped in a blanket
discreetly downwind.

Finally he moved back to the tomb,
going out only in the evening to follow
the sun into the West.

God's name in vain on his cracked and loamy lips.

SUSAN KOLODNY

Tsuneko—Psychiatric Medications Clinic

Along the north-south street, glass birds
leave their droppings green gold blue and silver,
they glint in the cold light, on the square flat stones.
Walk slowly, Tsuneko. Don't trouble the streams here
of air, the spirits of this place. Slowly, to the white room,
up narrow steps, do not touch the polished railing.
You did once and froze there. And could see
the melted horses, the screaming trees,
skulls in the windows, bones in the wind.
Go up to the strange wall with the small holes.
The woman there plugs them with cords, plugs, unplugs.
She will give you back your doctor's name.

These doctors dissolve from one into another
and never grow old, men into women, larger
into smaller, they no longer have names.
They give you blue pills, round pellets
to inflate and stay above the flood on—an island hillock,
a small boat at home.

They say come back the second of april the
eleventh of may. You nod, Tsuneko. You have nodded
here always never saying I do not understand.
A nod will release you out into the air,
among the green gold blue and silver droppings
of glass birds, with your pills, to return the day
they are gone the glass tube hollow as reeds.

Once you nodded and a new one said
Do you understand me and you said no.
Tell me how I can help you understand me. What do you call

today? You say the eighth month the sixth day.
Come again then on the ninth month the third day.

This you do, up the stairs to the white room,
not touching the polished railing lest you stick there
as you did once to the wood you clutched
and did not unstick even when you crossed the ocean
with the dark enemy soldier to live in this place
and have children who would leave you coming no more
on your birthday as your mother has not come
since the sky burned the horses melted your brother
turned to chalk your father to stone.

Here is the doctor, Tsuneko. From your bag
you give her the rose the voices told you
to bring her. Her face is a pond you have dropped a pebble in.
She looks at you and sees you there; you *are* there.
Then the melted horses and burnt trees flicker.
You say the Thank You the Good-bye you have learned to
and you go back out into the cold air the frozen light
the glass droppings of green gold blue and silver
the north-south street the square flat stones.

YUSEF KOMUNYAKAA

Salt

Lisa, Leona, Loretta?
She's sipping a milkshake
In Woolworths, dressed in
Chiffon & fat pearls.
She looks up at me,
Grabs her purse
& pulls at the hem
Of her skirt. I want to say
I'm just here to buy
A box of Epsom salt
For my grandmama's feet.
Lena, Lois? I feel her
Strain to not see me.
Lines are now etched
At the corners of her thin,
Pale mouth. Does she know
I know her grandfather
Rode a white horse
Through Poplas Quarters
Searching for black women,
How he killed Indians
& stole land with bribes
& fake deeds? I remember
She was seven & I was five
When she ran up to me like a cat
With a gypsy moth in its mouth
& we played doctor & house
Under the low branches of a raintree
Encircled with red rhododendrons.

We could pull back the leaves
& see grandmama ironing
At their wide window. Once
Her mother moved so close
To the yardman we thought they'd kiss.
What the children of housekeepers
& handymen knew was enough
To stop biological clocks,
& it's hard now not to walk over
& mention how her grandmother
Killed her idiot son
& salted him down
In a wooden barrel.

TED KOOSER

In the Basement of the Goodwill Store

In musty light, in the thin brown air
of damp carpet, doll heads and rust,
beneath long rows of sharp footfalls
like nails in a lid, an old man stands
trying on glasses, lifting each pair
from the box like a glittering fish
and holding it up to the light
of a dirty bulb. Near him, a heap
of enameled pans as white as skulls
looms in the catacomb shadows,
and old toilets with dry red throats
cough up bouquets of curtain rods.

You've seen him somewhere before.
He's wearing the green leisure suit
you threw out with the garbage,
and the Christmas tie you hated,
and the ventilated wingtip shoes
you found in your father's closet
and wore as a joke. And the glasses
which finally fit him, through which
he looks to see you looking back—
two mirrors which flash and glance—
are those through which one day
you too will look down over the years,
when you have grown old and thin
and no longer particular,
and the things you once thought
you were rid of forever
have taken you back in their arms.

The Riddle of Noah

You want to change your name. You're looking
for "something more suitable," words we can only guess
you've come by from television or teachers. All
your first-grade friends have names like Justin Mark
Caroline Emma or newly enrolled Xuan Loc
and yours, you sadly report, is Noah ... nothing.

Noah *Hodges,* your middle name isn't nothing
your mother, named Hodges, reproves, but you go on looking.
Next day you are somebody else: Adam Stinger! The clock
turns back to my brother, Edward Elias, whose quest
to be named for his father (living names are death marks
on a Jewish child) was fulfilled by a City Hall

clerk. Peter Jr. went gladly to school all
unblessed. The names that we go by are nothing
compared to the names we are called. *Christ killer!* they mocked
and stoned me with quinces in my bland-looking
suburb. Why didn't I tattle, resist? I guessed
I was guilty, the only kid on my manicured block

who didn't know how to genuflect as we lock-
stepped to chapel at noontime. I was in thrall,
the one Jewish girl in my class at Holy Ghost
convent school. Xuan Loc, which translates as something
magical and tender—Spring Bud, a way of looking
at innocence—is awarded the gold bookmark

for reading more chapter-books than Justin Mark
or Noah, who now has tears in his eyes. No lack
of feeling here, a jealous Yahweh is looking

over his shoulder hissing, Be best of all.
What can be done to ease him? Nothing
makes up for losing, though love is a welcome guest.

Spared being burned at the stake, being starved or gassed,
like Xuan Loc, Noah is fated to make his mark,
suffer for grace through good works, aspire to something.
Half-Jewish, half-Christian, he will own his name, will unlock
the riddle of who he is: only child, in equal
measure blessed and damned to be inward-looking,

always slightly aslant the mark, like Xuan Loc.
Always playing for keeps, for all or nothing
in quest of his rightful self while the world looks on.

STANLEY KUNITZ

The Flight of Apollo

Earth was my home, but even there I was a stranger. This mineral crust. I walk like a swimmer. What titanic bombardments in those old astral wars! I know what I know: I shall never escape from strangeness or complete my journey. Think of me as nostalgic, afraid, exalted. I am your man on the moon, a speck of megalomania, restless for the leap toward island universes pulsing beyond where the constellations set. Infinite space overwhelms the human heart, but in the middle of nowhere life inexorably calls to life. Forward my mail to Mars. What news from the Great Spiral Nebula in Andromeda and the Megallanic Clouds?

2

I was a stranger on earth.
Stepping on the moon, I begin
the gay pilgrimage to new
Jerusalems
in foreign galaxies.
Heat. Cold. Craters of silence.
The Sea of Tranquillity
rolling on the shores of entropy.
And, beyond,
the intelligence of the stars.

WENDY WILDER LARSEN

Learning the War

I never made friends faster.
We foreigners were learning the war,
cramming it in
breakfast, lunch and dinner.

We learned the abbreviations:
USAID, JUSPAI, MACV, DMZ,
ARVN, NLF, GVN.

We learned the names of battles:
Dien Bien Phu
Ashau Valley
Khe Sanh
Hamburger Hill
Firebase Mary Ann.

We peppered our speech
with militarese

with roger this
and roger that
with dust off
blown away and neutralize

to give us courage—
warriors painting our faces
before battle.

We learned to rate hamlets
praise Ruff-Puffs

recognize Kit Carson scouts
laugh at White Mice.

We learned it all
and we couldn't speak to anyone
when we got home.

DORIANNE LAUX

Prayer

Sweet Jesus, let her save you, let her take
your hands and hold them to her breasts,
slip the sandals from your feet, lay your body down
on sheets beaten clean against the fountain stones.
Let her rest her dark head on your chest,
let her tongue lift the fine hairs like a sword tip
parting the reeds, let her lips burnish
your neck, let your eyes be wet with pleasure.
Let her keep you from that other life, as a mother
keeps a child from the brick lip of a well,
though the rope and bucket shine and clang,
though the water's hidden silk and mystery call.
Let her patter soothe you and her passions
distract you, let her show you the light
storming the windows of her kitchen, peaches
in a wooden bowl, a small square of gray cloth
she has sewn to her skirt to cover the tear.
What could be more holy than the curve of her back
as she sits, her hands opening a plum.
What could be more sacred than her eyes,
fierce and complicated as the truth, your life
rising behind them, your name on her lips.
Stay there, in her bare house, the black pots
hung from pegs, bread braided and glazed
on the table, a clay jug of violet wine.
There is the daily sacrament of rasp and chisel,
another chair to be made, shelves to be hewn
clean and even and carefully joined
to the sun-scrubbed walls, a sharp knife

for carving odd chunks of wood into spoons
and toys for the children. Oh Jesus, close your eyes
and listen to it, the air is alive with bird calls
and bees, the dry rustle of palm leaves,
her distracted song as she washes her feet.
Let your death be quiet and ordinary.
Either life you choose will end in arms.

JON LAVIERI

The Autobiography of John Doe

as told to Miranda

He got hauled in
on a routine sweep for illegals,
and since he was a bachelor
with no particular fondness
for his career, saw no reason
to resist a strange and sudden urge
to play dumb for the immigration agents.
He threw everything
but the cash in his pocket
out the meat wagon window,
slept the next two nights in a chair
in a locked room at the INS.
Then they put him on a plane,
returning him to someone else's life,
anyone whose file needed closing.

There was a woman with a
hard bronze loveliness
waiting on the tarmac
when he landed. He would do,
she thought, understanding everything at once.

It struck him that her hands
were older than the rest of her.
We, her children, learned to call him Papa,
and she made love to him
as long as he kept pretending.
All of the village played along

for our sake, even though they remembered
the man he was not.
He never learned our language,
and somehow forgot the one he had before.

But he never treated anyone with undue cruelty,
and so was buried in the local graveyard
beside our mother. We remember
how sad he became toward the end
over failing to honestly love either world.

I now bring my children to see
where their grandmother lies,
and over there, the man who posed
as a man we all knew.

DON L. LEE

Gwendolyn Brooks

she doesn't wear
costume jewelry
& she knew that walt disney
was/is making a fortune off
false-eyelashes and that time magazine is the
authority on the knee/grow.
her makeup is total-real.

a negro english instructor called her:
    "a fine negro poet."
a whi-te critic said:
    "she's a credit to the negro race."
somebody else called her:
    "a pure negro writer."
johnnie mae, who's a senior in high school said:
    "she & langston are the only negro poets we've
    read in school and i understand her."
pee wee used to carry one of her poems around in his
    back pocket;
        the one about being cool. that was befo pee wee
        was cooled by a cop's warning shot.

into the sixties
a word was born . . . . BLACK
& with black came poets
& from the poet's ball points came:
black doubleblack purpleblack blueblack beenblack was
black daybeforeyesterday blackerthan ultrablack super
black blackblack yellowblack niggerblack blackwhi-te-man
blackerthanyoueverbes 1/4 black unblack coldblack clear

black my momma's blackerthanyourmomma pimpleblack fall
black so black we can't even see you black on black in
black by black technically black mantanblack winter
black coolblack 360degreesblack coalblack midnight
black black when it's convenient rustyblack moonblack
black starblack summerblack electronblack spaceman
black shoeshineblack jimshoeblack underwearblack ugly
black auntjimammablack, uncleben'srice black williebest
black blackisbeautifulblack i justdiscoveredblack negro
black unsubstanceblack.

and everywhere the
lady "negro poet"
appeared the poets were there.
they listened & questioned
& went home feeling uncomfortable/unsound & so-untogether
they read/re-read/wrote & re-wrote
& came back the next time to tell the
lady "negro poet"
how beautiful she was/is & how she had helped them
& she came back with:
        how necessary they were and how they've helped her.
the poets walked & as space filled the vacuum between them & the
lady "negro poet"
u could hear one of the blackpoets say:
        "bro, they been callin that sister by the wrong name."

LI-YOUNG LEE

Persimmons

In sixth grade Mrs. Walker
slapped the back of my head
and made me stand in the corner
for not knowing the difference
between *persimmon* and *precision.*
How to choose

persimmons. This is precision.
Ripe ones are soft and brown-spotted.
Sniff the bottoms. The sweet one
will be fragrant. How to eat:
put the knife away, lay down newspaper.
Peel the skin tenderly, not to tear the meat.
Chew the skin, suck it,
and swallow. Now, eat
the meat of the fruit,
so sweet,
all of it, to the heart.

Donna undresses, her stomach is white.
In the yard, dewy and shivering
with crickets, we lie naked,
face-up, face-down.
I teach her Chinese.
Crickets: *chiu chiu.* Dew: I've forgotten.
Naked: I've forgotten.
Ni, wo: you and me.
I part her legs,
remember to tell her
she is beautiful as the moon.

Other words
that got me into trouble were
fight and *fright, wren* and *yarn.*
Fight was what I did when I was frightened,
fright was what I felt when I was fighting.

Wrens are small, plain birds,
yarn is what one knits with.
Wrens are soft as yarn.
My mother made birds out of yarn.
I loved to watch her tie the stuff;
a bird, a rabbit, a wee man.

Mrs. Walker brought a persimmon to class
and cut it up
so everyone could taste
a *Chinese apple.* Knowing
it wasn't ripe or sweet, I didn't eat
but watched the other faces.

My mother said every persimmon has a sun
inside, something golden, glowing,
warm as my face.

Once, in the cellar, I found two wrapped in newspaper,
forgotten and not yet ripe.
I took them and set both on my bedroom windowsill,
where each morning a cardinal
sang, *The sun, the sun.*

Finally understanding
he was going blind,
my father sat up all one night

waiting for a song, a ghost.
I gave him the persimmons,
swelled, heavy as sadness,
and sweet as love.

This year, in the muddy lighting
of my parents' cellar, I rummage, looking
for something I lost.
My father sits on the tired, wooden stairs,
black cane between his knees,
hand over hand, gripping the handle.
He's so happy that I've come home.
I ask how his eyes are, a stupid question.
All gone, he answers.

Under some blankets, I find a box.
Inside the box I find three scrolls.
I sit beside him and untie
three paintings by my father:
Hibiscus leaf and a white flower.
Two cats preening.
Two persimmons, so full they want to drop from the cloth.

He raises both hands to touch the cloth,
asks, *Which is this?*

This is persimmons, Father.

Oh, the feel of the wolftail on the silk,
the strength, the tense
precision in the wrist.
I painted them hundreds of times
eyes closed. These I painted blind.

Some things never leave a person:
scent of the hair of one you love,
the texture of persimmons,
in your palm, the ripe weight.

PHILIP LEVINE

Soloing

My mother tells me she dreamed
of John Coltrane, a young Trane
playing his music with such joy
and contained energy and rage
she could not hold back her tears.
And sitting awake now, her hands
crossed in her lap, the tears start
in her blind eyes. The TV set
behind her is gray, expressionless.
It is late, the neighbors quiet,
even the city—Los Angeles—quiet.
I have driven for hours down 99,
over the Grapevine into heaven
to be here. I place my left hand
on her shoulder, and she smiles.
What a world, a mother and son
finding solace in California
just where we were told it would
be, among the palm trees and all-
night super markets pushing orange
back-lighted oranges at 2 A.M.
"He was alone," she says, and does
not say, just as I am, "soloing."
What a world, a great man half
her age comes to my mother
in sleep to give her the gift
of song, which—shaking the tears
away—she passes on to me, for now
I can hear the music of the world

in the silence and that word:
soloing. What a world—when I
arrived the great bowl of mountains
was hidden in a cloud of exhaust,
the sea spread out like a carpet
of oil, the roses I had brought
from Fresno browned on the seat
beside me, and I could have
turned back and lost the music.

LARRY LEVIS

The Morning After My Death

My body is a white thing in the sun, now.
It is not ashamed of itself,
Not anymore. Because today is
The morning after my death.
How little I have to say;
How little desire I have
To say it.

And these flies sleeping on doorsills
And hugging screens; and the child
Who has just run out of the house
After touching my body, who knows,
Suddenly, how heavy a dead man is . . .

What can the sun do but keep shining?
Even though I don't especially need it
Anymore, it shines on the palm fronds
And makes them look older,
The way someone who writes a letter,
And then tears it up, looks suddenly older.

2.
Far off, a band is playing Souza marches.
And as the conductor, in his sun stained
Uniform, taps his baton for silence, and all
Around him the foliage is getting greener,
Greener, like the end of things,
One of the musicians, resting
His trumpet on his knee, looks around

A moment, before he spits and puts his horn
Into his mouth, counting slowly.

And so I think of the darkness inside the horn,
How no one's breath has been able
To push it out yet, into the air,
How when the concert ends it will still
Be there, like a note so high no one
Can play it, or like the dried blood inside
A dead woman's throat, when the mourners
Listen, and there is nothing left but these flies,
Polished and swarming frankly in the sun.

TIMOTHY LIU

Thoreau

My father and I have no place to go.
His wife will not let us in the house—
afraid of catching AIDS. She thinks
sleeping with men is more than a sin,
my father says, as we sit on the curb
in front of someone else's house.
Sixty-four years have made my father
impotent. Silver roots, faded black
dye mottling his hair make him look
almost comical, as if his shame
belonged to me. Last night we read
Thoreau in a steak house down the road
and wept: *If a man does not keep pace
with his companions, let him travel
to the music that he hears, however
measured or far away.* The orchards
are gone, his village near Shanghai
bombed by the Japanese, the groves
I have known in Almaden—apricot,
walnut, peach and plum—hacked down.

MARGARET LLOYD

The Simplest and the Hardest

I prepare for you the way I plan
for yearly visits from my brother's son—
deaf from birth, now a man.

I take the *Joy of Signing* down,
drive left hand on the wheel, name
with fingers of my right: *mountain,*

hawk, grass, cattail, flock, rain,
the world I see along the road. Words
unused, the way we never talk of *shame,*

regret. I sign and mouth the names of birds
for practice, recall and challenge limits
of my skill with him. We'll strain, beleaguered

by what we cannot say. And I admit
exaggeration replaces subtlety.
V's, signed with both hands moving, exploit

the complex truth, when all is *very, very. . . .*
But something does come through. I make a fist,
draw a circle on my breast for *sorry,*

feel my beating heart. Sounds I resist
come from his yearning throat. The voice of a man
who has never heard a human voice insists—

shocking, strange, reminding me that human
voices are only imitations of sounds
heard from birth. I know the more I strain

to read the signs, the less I understand
both the simplest facts we have to learn
and the hardest. Like the relief of hands

allowed to be still as well as the heart
which closes and opens when he departs.

GERALD LOCKLIN

The Stranger

We were building a fort
of cardboard boxes
in the narrow, grassless backyard
when the faceless man stood
in the driveway in the sun
his hands in his trench coat pockets
watching us
and he never went away.

Yesterday
I stood in the driveway
in my oldest trench coat
watching the neighborhood children
build a cardboard fort.

JOAN LOGGHE

Insomnia Litany

I am a Jew among sunflowers, a Jew
among stars. I am a Jew with allergies
in the night with a voice of pollen.
I am a Jew among tortillas and refried
beans, a Jew among Virgin of Guadalupe
candles, it took fourteen to just survive
the winter. I am a Jew among crosses,
even the compass on the dash makes
a sort of statement. I am a Jew
among bankers and grocery clerks.

I wear clothes like a Jew wears clothing.
I eat the foods a Jew eats. I pay bills
like a Jew and like a Jew I lie down,
thanking and worrying, praising and sighing.
All my days I will be a Jew. And my nights
among the other definitions of myself.
I will chew like a Jew. I will purchase
stamps in rural post offices. When the man
says, "I jewed 'em down," I will pleasantly say,
"Be careful. You never know who you're talking to.
I am a Jew." I will walk back to my car
like a Jew, feeling the strain of having
to speak my piece among strangers in line
at Santa Cruz.

I find my way back to the old ladies
from Europe, schlepping their groceries
home in a cart. I make jokes like a Jew.
And then my husband, who loves me like a Jew

loves, belying my mother's weekly speech
that Jewish men make the best husbands,
wraps around me and holds me like a human.
And I love him and sleep most humanely,
all night engraved in a landscape of ghosts,
the oy oy oy of love. I sleep the sleep
of the unlabeled. I sleep a circumcized sleep.

ROBERT HILL LONG

The Conspiracy

The Cambodian kids speak English faster,
better than any other kids on the block
and all three bang my door the third
hopeful time since noon: Seth home now?

Not yet, not yet, no. Away they sprint,
barefoot on the flagstone walk
though it's November: wild geese last week,
this week the B-52s homing in on Chicopee

on dry-runs so low I see shark-teeth
painted under their black clown-noses.
It's touch-and-go all day, those bombers,
regular as these kids: who bang, now, to ask

can they attack my big leaf-pile?
Up they fling maple shrapnel—then I hear
mother-noise, Cambodian. Ordering
her kids out of my leaves and home, probably.

On her porch she ducks the roar
of the B-52: a bow to old terror domesticated
to what? a polite fear that I'll call
welfare cops for Cambodian leaf-pile vandalism?

Two kids already she's renamed
for saint and martyr—Paul, Christina—,
already bought them baseball jackets
and drills them in English, manners, quickness

as though to head off the schoolyard hate
we both know their gold faces will attract.

She's let me teach them to bunt and steal second,
turn them into ghosts full of trick or treat,

but her folk-dance of immigrant dread
—wince and bow to neighbor-with-leafpile,
welfare officer, bomber that bombed
her youth to moon-mud— makes me wince and bow

on my small porch, and wave to show I know
how that dance goes. One hand on the door,
one foot inside the house where each night
America surrenders to Cambodia,

she gives a wave so underhanded
I almost miss the small quick smile.
The smile that translates *all-clear, truce,*
OK, hello. That says the kids can stay.

THOMAS LUX

Bodo

> History is largely made up of Bodos.
> —Eileen Power, *Medieval People*

We could weep for him
but we won't: the man
who scythed and ground the oats
but ate no bread; who pumped one oar
among thousands at Lepanto, ocean
up to his clavicles and rising; who
in countless numbers served as food
for countless fish. The man,
or sometimes woman, three or four rows back
in the crowd (listless, slack-mouthed),
who lined the street when an army,
depleted or fat with loot, came home;
or the man behind such columns,
who gathered the dung
to sell or to pick for seeds. All the pig farmers,
rat catchers, charcoal burners, tanners
in their stink, root diggers living
in the next village over from the smallest village;
who thickened their soup with sawdust
or meal gathered from dirt
around the grindstone.
Your great-great-etc.-uncle Fedor who never spoke
but in grunts, who beat his spavined horse,
who beat his rented field
for millet, sorghum, who ate a chicken once a year,
who could not read

nor even sign an X; the slaves
unnamed who never made it
to the slavers, buzzards' bait,
or did not survive the crossing
if they did. All the Bodos
who stood on docks with breaking backs
and did not wave
and did not know Marco Polo
was setting out again; the zealous priest
eleventh on the list
to seek out Prester John; the convict-colonists
who preferred the gaol at home
but had no choice. The slug-pickers;
the sailors who bailed the bilge water
hanging by their heels; the doughboy
dead of typhus before he wrote a letter home;
the man who thought he pleased a minor Nazi
with an act of small servility
and was proud and told his wife and son;
who lost a leg and half his face for his king,
and then was cheated on his pension
and was not bitter. The man, the woman, who hanged
or burned for nothing
and did not weep, or, tortured, confessed
too fast or less; who praised his slop
in which a fish head floated . . .

JENNIFER MARTELLI

Mal'Occhio

The red pepper hangs from a nail
above the back doorjamb, and the totem

inside its belly laughs—he is rich, hunchback
and can trick the Devil. I take careful

stock, touch my stoneware
plates, the ones with fired apples

on ivory paint. The white ceramic bowl
with spare change and spare keys. Unfinished

crewelwork blessing in its bag. The needles. Books.
Here is where I pray at night,

the foot of my bed. This is my coverlet,
undyed muslin and clean. And under it,

a brutal thing, an ugly girl,
God-blessed, left alone. The ceiling

shines white, drinking up what little
moon can come through: a cup of milk, enough

for one night. That's it. No one wants
anything of mine. I don't even make

a shadow on the wall. The bedsprings barely
creak as I pull the pure cotton

close and tight, gift-wrapped, like a nun.
Muffled goodness. Beneficent abstraction. Snuffed flame.

DIONISIO D. MARTÍNEZ

Pain

for Armando Valladares

We all expected to see you lame.
Some *wanted* to see you lame.
When you walked toward us,
we imagined you crawling. It was
like waiting for a train that suddenly
turns into a wolf: it howls
as it runs into the station, its eyes
blind you like headlights, you step
into its mouth as if it were a car, you
think of tunnels and the next stop
as you're being devoured: you expected
a train and can't imagine anything else.
We waited with a wheelchair for a man who
could've used a new pair of shoes.
We asked the obvious questions:
if half a life of torture really
softens the bones until the body falls
like a ruined shack, if rebuilding
the shack is worth the trouble. And when
someone mentioned pain, the word rising
from its metaphors, you tried to laugh.

Your mouth opened like a small wound.

WILLIAM MATTHEWS

Old Folsom Prison

This could be Scotland: a crag and far below
the froth-marled river. Where is the stag,
the laird, where are the baying hounds?

Welcome instead to Hotel California.
Johnny Cash sang right there, in Graystone
Chapel, and from the blue, disconsolate

congregation he drew, like blood, whoops
and yelps enough to flood the place.
Rapists rose; and arsonists; and the man

who drew five life sentences, without
parole, for vehicular homicide
(a mother and four kids), to be served

consecutively, rose also; as did
murderers enough to still all breath
in a small town; and armed robbers; and

sellers of dope to your children and mine,
and earlier, perhaps, to you and me.
And when Cash sang that he'd stabbed

a man just to watch him die, their shout
rose like so many crows you'd wonder where
there was room for air, if you were there.

JANET MCADAMS

Leaving the Old Gods

I.

The people who watch me hang my coat
on a peg at the office don't even know
about that other life,
the life when there was you, *it*,
however briefly. To them my body
is a fact casual as the weather.
I could tell them:
That day it rained
the way it rains in the New World.
Leaves struck the window like daggers.
I didn't think about *God*
but the ones we used to worship
the ones who want your heart still
beating, who load you with gold
and lure you to sleep
deep in the cenote.

II.

A girl, he said, and I nodded
though we couldn't have known.
I would have left him then
for ten thousand pesos.
I don't know what world you inhabit,
swimming there, baby, not-baby,
part of my body, not me,
swept aside like locks of hair
or toenail parings.
It's ten years today
and you who were never alive

pull a face in the leaves
of the jacaranda, the only tree
that lives outside my window.
It must be your voice
whistling through the office window,
though I can't understand your words.
Comfort or accusation,
I can't understand your words.

MEKEEL MCBRIDE

The Knife-Thrower's Wife

The knife-thrower's wife stands
stranded in danger's glittery geography.
A paper heart is pinned in sequin
to her breast. She would be afraid
if she could see her husband caress
each knife, mouth her name before aiming.

But the spot-light sews her eyes shut.
"Slut," he says to himself, "you whore."
Now she hears them coming, a sound
like bees, a sound of bullets. She
wonders if there is a war somewhere.
Applause. A held-breath pause.

He places his blindfold carefully. He aims
as close to her heart as he can. And then
it is over. She steps forward, sees
her silhouette set out by ice-pick,
sword, all manner of sharp things. She
joins hands with her husband. They bow.

She sees he loves his knives more than
he loves life: his, hers, it doesn't matter.
This is what makes her take her place
again and again, glad for the knives
that need her, that wait to surround her
like a crowd of adoring suitors.

VICTORIA MCCABE

The People at the Pay Telephone

A husband or a lover has run this one out
In robe and curlers; this one
Has had his money stolen at the airport,

And this one has lost his mind altogether,
And dials repeatedly "Information."
—They are a decidedly 20th century lot,

Jingling their dimes, standing around,
Stamping against the March wind, looking
Confused, the complicated wires and metallic

Cords tying them up. They reach only
And repeatedly buzzings and bleepings, Wrong
Numbers, Missed Connections, Disconnections,

Unlisted, Changed Numbers, Deposit-Please-
A-Million-Dollars, Busy, Busy, Busy.
They are singularly unable to talk back

To the recorded voice that repeats itself:
We are unable, We are unable ... They've heard
It before, their ears read with cold, or sun,

Or both, shivering, or sweating, exposed ...
They alone in the 20th century here must face
Such elemental battles, the rest

Of the world tonight sitting around
A swimming pool, or fireplace, the rest of the world
Eating fine food, talking to people.

WALTER MCDONALD

After the Noise of Saigon

If where we hunt defines us,
then stalking this steep hillside
dark with spruce makes sense,

more than the dreams I've floundered in
for years, trying to fathom signs
all night and wading ashore

disgusted. Switches dripping sap
keep flipping me when I glance
over my shoulder for spoor

I might have missed. Evergreen
needles sting when I swing my head
face-forward for clues. Isn't this

the strangest nightmare of all,
knowing my aim with a bow
is no better at twenty yards

than forty? But here I am, alone
with a cougar I've stalked for hours,
climbing until I'm dizzy.

These blue trees have nothing
and all to do with what I'm here for
after the noise of Saigon,

the simple bitter sap that rises in me
like bad blood I need to spill
out here alone in the silence

of deep woods, far from people I know
who see me as a friend, not some damned
madman stumbling for his life.

JOE-ANNE MCLAUGHLIN

Black Irish Blues

1. "You mighty beautiful, but you gotta die someday."
                                        —Traditional Blues

Already this tremor in my hands—
like my father's toward the end
when he couldn't steady his fork
long enough to get his food down clean
let alone get down on his bass,
or so his common-law widow said.
It was another one of those last
chances the Musicians' Union gave him,
and I don't know who got his bass
out of Bob's Friendly Loaner for him
that time, unless it was Buzzy
the trumpet player who is dead now
too, they say. It was a beauty
of a beast anyway. Grand,
not like the electric jobs
these glamor guys play; only unhandy
as a coffin or a crucifix to haul.
But we hauled her, the twelve blocks
uptown to the Black Orchid. Had to,
and in the pouring rain, because
same as always Daddy'd shot
the cab fare on stuff. But wasn't he fine,
really in there, those first two sets?
The way he played that box
made me think if a penis could speak
it would speak in Bass. Only

then he began missing, worse and worse
(nodding out, is what they call it),
until midway through the third set he crashed—
bass, stool, and all—smack down
on the bouncer's classy date.
Awful. Sure. Only same as always
nobody could afford any trouble.
They packed us into a taxi, and Daddy
was straight enough by then, at least,
to cry. And it wasn't long after, I
got sentenced to the Good Shepherd Home
for Troubled Girls, meaning "wayward," and next
I heard he was busted in Miami
for possession. Then he was dead. Now
already his tremor's shaking me,
the single record he left.

2. Elegy: Out of the Pit, Like Music

It didn't rain. It couldn't
gloom as it had his agelong days;
rather the day bloomed and flew,
bluebirds and bluets on every grave.
And shine? A few shades brighter
than ever he could stand, or any of us
when low can bear. Take
the bluest moments of your life,
one Good Friday after another,
Stormy Monday, The Second Flood,
and no change forecast. You knew
(and from lick one) where his music
came from; and I don't mean

from the heart, not that,
nor from no music school either,
but scared up from the glands, like sweat,
and from the tear ducts
and from the dried-out cock
doomed yet blowing against all sense
kisses back at puckering death.
You knew, or rather your own doomed
innards knew, and the knowing
trembled through you and ached
so that you didn't know whether
to clap or to gasp.
Understand, for one thus damned,
death is nearly a resurrection.
Understand, it killed me just the same.

PABLO MEDINA

The Exile

He returned to grass two feet tall
around the house, a rope dangling
from the oak, an absence of dogs.
The year had neither ended nor begun,
the sun had yawned away the rain
and worms were drying on the ground.

Memories floated down from the trees: cane fields,
the smokehouse and its hanging meats,
breeze of orange and bamboo, a singing at dawn.

"Will you be with me?"
The voice came from the river. The jasmine
bloomed in the garden, he hiding,
he sweating under the moon
wanting to say I will I will and more.

There were stones all over the yard smelling of time.
He picked a few, threw them down the well
and listened to the water swallowing.

It made him smaller. He walked out the gate
and closed it behind him, wiped the sweat from his eyes,
felt his feet settling on the road.

ASKOLD MELNYCZUK

The Usual Immigrant Uncle Poem

He feared money so much he was known
to shake and sweat in line at the register.

Once, they say, he broke down and wept.
And it seemed funny to us at Christmas

when he wore
his sister-in-law's underwear

on his head.
But we did not know

how it had been
back in Pereyaslav

or whatever other place
I never saw, and so

can't care for, really,
where they took his father,

a famous judge and orator,
and stood him against the wall

and so on.
Still, that doesn't quite explain the money.

CHRISTOPHER MERRILL

Erosion

Parachuting into the desert is a quiet arrival,
but I've seen hillsides become alive with snakes.
  —Dr. Gerald Crenshaw, *Albuquerque Journal*

Past the salt flats, the grave of the sea, the sky
Divers in a free fall, twisting and turning,
Like stones dropped in water—they heard only the whine
Of the wind, the drone of the plane flying home.

Their chutes erupted like an argument,
And up they floated, up—then down. They saw smoke
Rising from the last city, houses reclining
On the worn benches of the mountains, and rain

Evaporating in midair. They carried
Their own clouds into the desert, the rippling
Cloth and cords trailing them like debts, like children
And beliefs. And once they landed on the mesa,

Splashing into the sand, they felt the past
Dissolve. So they praised the action of their chutes
Settling, like snow, over the stunted trees,
Over all the shrubs and flowers they would have

To name. They praised the ebbing wind, the silence,
And the taste of their own salt. They praised a cactus
In the shape of a cross . . . Yet it was a dead place
To these disciples of the future, these

Pilgrims gathering potsherds and petrified
Chunks of wood. They damned the dry gullies. Damned

The heat rooted in the red earth and the hidden
Barbs of the prickly pear . . . Then it began.

In arroyos, on hillsides: a hissing and
A heaving, like the sea. Or was this just
The memory of the sea? They waved at the sky,
They scanned birds' nests, gopher holes, anthills, ants:

Nothing. One laced up his boots. Another grabbed
A hatchet. A third tried to pray. Soon waves
Of diamondbacks were breaking on the mesa,
Eroding the shore beneath the nomads' feet.

Enduring Witness, the Mosques of Kattankudi

Muhammad wheels us through
these incisive narrow lanes,
the same the Tigers took
grim, methodical, and quick
to yet another keening mosque—
a plaque inscribes each name and age,
one hundred three in all, the youngest six.

An ancient man, survived, displays his wound
and shrugs—Allah's will, Muhammad says,
a pillar saved the old Imam and him.
The walls, the floor, the splintered struts
all bear witness to the old man's memory . . .
Prostrate, pious forehead to the floor,
what could he see or know
who only recollects a sudden fusillade,
a hundred strangled prayers in stricken throats,
and then as now a silence
punctuating groans of brute mortality.

Outside, a gaggle of small boys—
one quickly darts to touch my arm
like counting coup.
His buddies giggle. Muhammad smiles.

At Muhammad's home a photo record
of the massacres in grisly Kodachrome.
I set aside these documents.
My witness cannot bear so much.

Now, though curfew's drawing on,
custom's mercy mandates tea.

Muhammad's wife quietly attends
with sugared cashews, treacle cakes, vatalappan
then, backing off, stands smiling by.
The children, curious, are let in.
First of course the son, age six,
then the slightly elder girl, shy
but strangely bolder than the boy.
Then cousins, uncles, aunts
until at last another ancient man . . .

I turn away and see the photos
open on the couch and turn away again.
Back at the mosque, marked by low stone walls,
the dead are filed in pebbled graves.
Meanwhile we are, too like the Tigers, quick—
our fragile witness borne
upon those durable imperatives
grace and hospitality.

JOSEPH MILLAR

Midlife

She's slim and seems distracted, the social worker
who visits my apartment, who wants to know
why my ten-year-old was alone on New Year's Eve
when the cops came through the door.

His mother was drunk, I say, and I was up north
with my girlfriend who doesn't want any more kids.
Would she like a cup of tea?
We do have some problems here, I know—
as I force-feed old newspapers into the trash—
but hopefully nothing too unseemly,
no disarray that can't be explained.

I want to say I've tried
to find another way to live,
away from the electric metal wires
that whisper to me in the afternoons,
the snake dreams that follow after,
uncoiling slowly in my sleep,
and the supermarkets where I go unconscious,
humming to myself and staring, minutes at a time,
at the olives and loaves of bread.

There's not much to show for all this:
four rooms, a dented Olds, tattered pictures
of Che Guevara and Muhammed Ali,
the Sixties with their fire and music scattered
highway cinders in the wind.
Does the state offer therapy for aging single fathers?
Is it all right to smoke?
Would she like to step into the back where it's dark

and fuck, standing up amid the laundry?
She smiles vaguely, hands me her card,
says she won't need to return.

Later I think this must be what it is
to get older. My knee hurts getting up
from the couch. Past fifty, can't work like I used to,
and my chest hairs are turning gray.
I'm angry with my son, now quietly asleep,
for needing help with everything: homework,
breakfast, rinsing the shampoo from his hair;
and sad, as I gather his small raincoat,
the baseball hat saying Surf's Up,
hang them over a chair, and start washing the pot
of day-old spaghetti we ate for dinner.

I listen to Miles with the lights off,
knowing the phone won't ring any more
and too tired to shower. I listen to my breath
leave and return, rain falling
into the cold trackless night,
and the wind in the trees outside
like someone passing.

DAVID MURA

The Blueness of the Day

1 Mizuno in Paris (1947)

It happened in an instant:

On the ridge, shells gutted up dirt and smoke,
a hundred mouths gaping at once . . . In that streaming,

through leafless woods rinsed with light,

thirty yards ahead, Shig aimed;
at this high whine, palpable as a spear

drilled through my eardrum, I hurled my weight to

earth. I still see my body arched like that, leaping,
as if I were somehow there

and not there, freed from myself . . .

———

I envied Shig. Whenever he entered a church,
in Rome, Naples, Paris, something
spoke to him, not about the strangeness

of living on earth, but some magical
promise, whatever it is
a clever boy sees in a broken toy.

In camp, our families were stuck
in the same barracks, separated by sheets:
snores, arguments, night noises of

our parents, war clips on the radio flooded
our dreams. That day we signed up with
the guards in the towers, we held the flag

to our hearts, staring in disbelief and wonder.
Shig was smiling, the stupid fuck.
But then, so was I, so was I . . .

———

It was all so predictable, so mechanical:
Like the way mother would raise her
cleaver, crunch its blade through the chicken's

joints, searing the limbs. Or the way,
seconds earlier, she drained its neck
in the dirt, thumbing blood from

the spongy windpipe, squeezing out its
wheezy squawk. It's like that German boy,
he was a boy, really, his straw colored hair,

ruddy translucent skin, the way he stared
at me, my bayonet in his belly, at me,
as if he'd suddenly discovered his one true

connection to the world. I can see his face
when I close my eyes, smell the rain flashing near
the Arno, thunder that seemed to shake

the fields of green wet wheat, like
girls tossing salt spray from their hair.
—Yes, I never felt more alive . . .

———

"*Okaa-san,* life is glorious here. Death
too. In the mirror I see the lines of bewilderment

that creased your face

as *otoo-san* stumbled each night
in the barracks, mumbling *sakura, sakura* . . .

Sometimes I think of what my hands have done,

what my eyes have seen,
and none of it connects to that face, staring back at me,

its smooth dark skin: I am sick of being

decent, dependable, Japanese . . ."
—Each night I write this letter;

each night it comes back: *Sender Unknown.*

———

Once I worked with my father
in the orange groves. Frost
was coming that night,
and we set out smudge pots, smoke
rising amid the wet leaves.
We were too hurried to speak, lighting
and laying them down, row on row.
I recall the black chortles of the crickets,
the bull frog in the ditch,
and the light at the tip of my father's cigar,
bobbing in the dark. The frost
never came, the oranges were saved,
hanging there, heavy
and round as breasts
'the day we moved out, the early

light lifting mist from the fields,
their green shade. Mother carried our lunch
in a *furoshiki*, Ginny her doll,
and the smell of *shoyu* was still
in the hall as I walked out the door.
I remember we said nothing, knew
nothing could be said. We
left the brass Buddha in the basement.
Who could we sell it to?
When father stepped towards the car,
he stepped across the morning
sun, and his body turned
to light, and I knew I hated him, his sharp
commands, *"Hayaku, hayaku . . ."*
his useless tongue. And then,

then the gates opened.

———

Shig's letter scatters on the floor. It started
with a story I'd heard before: How, when he set off,
his father took him by the shoulders

—he paid no attention to the guards at the gate—
"This is your country. Make me proud."
(Mine spat at me: "Bakka, when they let me out, then

I'll sign the oath.") Well, Shig did come home, only
one arm was gone, and after they'd feasted
on *tempura* and *sake*, after they'd laughed themselves drunk,

the father took Shig to the *ofuro*, helped him in,
and began, slowly, gently, lathering the stump,
the back where black peppers of shrapnel worked themselves

197

out like points of a pencil. All the while
he sang a Japanese lullaby, one
Shig recalled from childhood . . .

—What is it I can't believe?
In the prairie grass, on the hill outside
of camp, we buried a few Issei

and a baby, flung like a seed
in the maw of earth. Last night
I saw my mother there, laying out

plates of *teriyaki, gohan, mochi.*
She arranged four sets of *hashi,*
and I thought it was for our family,

but when she turned and looked
back at me, I knew: It was
oshoshiki. Food for the dead . . .

———

"Okaa-san, you ask me why I will not come home:
But we only explain suffering to console

ourselves . . . It is chance, not God

or *Dharma,* which placed me here, wounded,
surviving, possessing nothing. *Okaa-san,*

there were camps here

so much more hideous than ours:
Our suffering so small it might have seemed

paradise to these. *Okaa-san,*

even in my worst rages
I could not slash the Mona Lisa or the sinners of Caravaggio—

What allowed me to do what I have done? . . .

Okaa-san, think of this space between us
as the wall where messages

are scraped out between two prisoners . . ."

—The words vanish.
I begin again. . . .

———

I walk the streets to keep awake.
The empty parks, pigeons, strollers, gutters
streaming with rain. Patisseries, flower stalls,

gendarmes, bicycles, boucheries. Stones
in the cemeteries with legendary names.
Bridges, grey and rain-beaten, arched

above the Seine. Poles marking an angle
on the banks. Is it better to say, "I am suffering,"
than "This landscape is ugly"? Each evening

an alarm goes off. I start walking again.
When I see them beneath a street light,
or lounging in doors, their perfume

already trudging up a stairway to this small room,
I know I am so far past bitterness
I must be bitterness itself.

Near morning, in a tiny room in Pigalle,
I'll rise, dress, the smell of her submission
on my cheeks, a pile of cigarettes

left by the bed. And for a few minutes, I'll keep
her face beneath me, almost dead, almost
frightened of whatever she sees there:

I've thought so often it's my skin, the folds
of my eyes, the alien energy thrashing her thighs,
but no, it's just my face, that implacable mask . . .

PETER E. MURPHY

The New Boy

Crossing Brooklyn Ferry from Staten Island
did not close the doors of the orphanage inside him.
On that boat he studied Casper the Friendly Ghost
and ate a hot dog and coke, the first supper of a life
he hoped not to suffer.

Crossing the Halloween Narrows that seamed
the night as if it were a border, he hoped to please
this new family, please their mint blue car
that drove him to the ferry from the school
for boys that darkened when he needed light.

He inhaled the salt breeze and drank his coke
and thought of the ghost that could not make friends
of the living by being what he was, which was dead.
He had to be heroic instead, the way little boys are not.
Where had Casper lived on Earth? he wondered.

How did he die? Why didn't he return to people
who loved him? He wondered too, if he would frighten
those who saw the deadness within him.
Is there a home where boys could learn to live
within their bodies? Where he could learn to live

in this new family? Would they keep him if he fails,
or throw him out to wander the streets of Brooklyn
begging for food or coins or love? Must he rattle
through these homes forever, pleading for someone
to play with, someone mean enough to take him in?

D. NURKSE

Olmos

A man walks a dusty road
dragging a suitcase.
Sometimes he looks back
and sees a shallow rut
wavering beside his footprints.
A dog howls behind a fence.
The man stops and says: shush.
The dog shuts up.
It has never heard such longing.
Olmos: the village of exile.
The guards are sitting on barrels
playing with creased cards.
My father has brought them
grandmother's lace, a pocket watch,
the locket with the child's tresses,
the diary locked with a gold key.
The visors evaluate these souvenirs
with one eye on their cards.
Olmos: a cider mill,
a tavern, a few porches.
A girl on a swing
watches my father
severely from several heights.
Suddenly she scuffs her heels
and runs through a red gate.
A man comes out—a real father—
and stares at the stranger
and spits: *Nothing,*
and shouts back at the cinched curtain:

Nothing to be afraid of.
Through the half-shut kitchen door
the smell of bread
reaches like a hand
that will mould me out of ashes.

NAOMI SHIHAB NYE

At Mother Teresa's

Finally there are enough people to hug!
A room of two-year-olds with raised arms . . .
we swing them into the air,
their grins are windows
in a city of crumbling walls.
One girl stays in the corner
crouched over her shoes.
Hard to keep shoes in this world,
people steal them, they walk away.
Her flaming hair is a house
she lives in all alone.
When I touch it she looks up,
suspicious, then lifts
a stub of chalk from her shoe.
Makes three jagged lines on the floor.
Can I read? I nod rapidly,
imagining *love me, love me, yes,*
but she is too alone to believe it.
Her face closes. I will never guess.

Calcutta

CAROLE SIMMONS OLES

For the Drunk

Where the river cleaves
our city from theirs
I watch from the sidewalk at 10 A.M.
him dart in front of the ranch wagon
which rocks to a stop
as he bends, disappears
behind the front fender

muttering, scoops up a handful
of something, covers it
with the dome of his palm,
zigzags onto the pavement
where the wind yanks
off his hat and drops it in traffic.

I'm reading his back
Santucci Bros. Contractor
wondering is it safe
to walk close when he

unlids what almost killed him—
two black bars in a yellow down face,
the most lost, puzzled duckling
that ever wanted its mama.

I hand him his hat.

STEVE ORLEN

Androgyny

Just when you thought it safe enough
To enter the water clean as a knife, after the kids
Have been stuffed and quieted with picnic lunch
And bided the requisite hour
Building castles in the sand, there she is,

Or he is. It's a man.
Can't we all tell by the feet and hands
And the dark stubbling under the cheeks?

He's wearing a woman's fashionably snug
Two-piece bathing suit. His hair lush, curly, black,
Blooms over the shoulders, and further down, such breasts . . .

All noise along the beach swells
Like a sudden wave, then stops.

To be both man and woman—
In all of us that potency, like a thousand
Messages into a thousand bottles
Returned, on the tides, with the answer . . .

No. Rather, you imagine the late-night
Twisting conversations, and try to imagine
Sharp pain of depilation, weekly hormone shots,
And before the mirror the endless practice,

Like this, like that, like this.
And then the breasts, truly wondrous,
Bobbing in the air for all to see.

And then, of course, the knife . . .

Two shapely, bathing-suited women grasp his arm
On either side. The three of them are laughing
Over something private. The grown-ups

Can't help themselves but stare. Two kids
Look down as the water takes away the sand,
Making moats of castles they've been playing in.

Then little Rebecca needs soothing,
And someone's sunburnt back needs creaming,
And a striped beach ball resumes its arc
Between that teenage boy and the other, *slap, slap,*

And the faint sound of derisive laughter,
And you in your simple singular flesh
Take off leaping toward the common water
Which cannot distinguish one sex from the other.

SIMON J. ORTIZ

On late-night television, two U.S. scientists talk about why the U.S., Russia, Japan, and several European nations have sent up satellite probes to photograph Halley's Comet, pass through its tail, see it up close. The scientists both agree it is "for the tremendous prestige" that would accrue to the nation to actually get there, to acquire information, and be the first to answer the unknown. That's all. One of the scientists says, "It costs as much as one B-1 bomber." Prestige, national standing, power. That's all.

In one of my short stories, an elder who's a grandfather asks, "And then will they know?"

The Possibility

> The old man could have told them.
> His grandson explained to him what was happening.
> "See those astronauts, Grandpa," he said,
> pointing to the TV screen. "They're on the moon
> to find out what's up there, to find the origin
> of life, where and how things all began."
> The old man couldn't believe it,
> and he couldn't believe his grandson talking,
> talking like the scientists who didn't know.
> He thought about stone, water, fire, and air.
> And he had to believe it was possible—some men
> didn't know or had forgotten
>
> > stone
> >
> > water
> >
> > fire
> >
> > air.
>
> He couldn't believe it, but it was possible.

ELISE PASCHEN

Two Standards

—at a Native Writers' Conference in Norman, Oklahoma

Joan's one eighth. I'm a quarter.
When we walk into Billy's
I want to look like her,
full Osage. "You wouldn't find
an Indian here," she tells me,
"if not for the conference."

And the cigar-chewing driver
shuttling in from the Will
Rogers Airport confides:
"I never seen so many
Indians all in one spot."
The bar's packed like a bar

should be. Joan shows me off,
introducing her friends
to a light-haired, East Coast-
educated outsider
whose mother, Betty Tallchief,
is Oklahoma's pride.

"At that table are some
Osages you should meet."
They know my relatives
in Fairfax, though they come
from Pawhuska, Pawnee.
Angela says the Tallchiefs,

the keepers of the drum,
will host the Osage dances

next June. "Will you join us?
You'll be given your Osage
name." Even though my grandmother
Tallchief's daughters became

famous as ballet dancers,
she displayed photographs
of my mother and aunt
when they were twelve, eleven
in Osage ceremonial dress,
performing at a powwow.

My mother said her father's
mother taught her those dances.
I say, when asked, I never wanted
to dance, but here, in Billy's
with the jukebox repeating
the Beatles' "Twist and Shout,"

all I want is to dance
and to adopt my mother's
Osage name "Wa-Xthe-thon-ba":
"Two Standards." All I want
is to return to Oklahoma
and answer Angela *"Yes,"*

though New York City's half
a continent away.
I am my mother's daughter,
"Two Standards," and tonight,
forgetting my given name,
I will take that ancestral one.

RICARDO PAU-LLOSA

Paredón

Staring down the mountainous wall,
I imagine my ear against the suicidal
waves as if the sea itself were a shell
against my cheek. The wall hoists
the sound of the waves to the parapet.
A tourist atop el Morro in San Juan,
I squint across the harbor entrance
to see a tiny ruined house, half
a stone shelter once still lumbering
among the surf-singed rocks. It is called
Isla de Cabras, the Island of Goats.

It was a leper colony during colonial times,
and now, nesting among the blackened
flanks and crannies, facing down the cobalt
horizon and the colossus who partners the bay,
it merely marks a torn page of island history.
Who among the heavy with pain, the ragged
in moment had heard of glory?
How did they ponder the flagging galleons
and the Dutch volleys, the native fears
and the pirates' rage?
The goats were guarded by their sores.
No one's plunder or slaves, not even
to themselves treasure, they must have sat
atop these rocks that shine like dropped jewels
to watch the comedy of battles and trade,
owning the world the only way it can be owned,
in unlosable distance.

They were free to stalk the Isla's
narrow cell much as inmates in Havana's Morro
have always done. Across the bay from that castle
is the capital, walled and brilliant, unlike
San Juan, a hub for flotas and armies,
cathedrals and books, all of which mattered little.
Cuba's lepers are the free. They are sent to the Morro
to rot or to be lined against its wet, green walls
and rehearse their executions before finally being shot.
For centuries the scene has not changed.
The families wait to visit what's left of the living
inside the Morro. At home the son or wife bolt from sleep
when the slightest noise could be dawn's execution.
In 1959 and 60 and 61 and since the mob begged
firing squad for those it neither knew or tried.
"Paredón! Paaredón! PaaareDON! PaaaareDOOON!"
The screamed word twists out of its own body
and lifts up the castle walls.
Cursed island who has never known its sick from itself.

MARCIA PELLETIERE

Under Her Crib

In the Yiddish song a goat danced under
Ehteleh's crib, to rock it gently.

Ehteleh is Esther now; at seventy-nine,
small and frail in her hospital bed,
she recalls a strange feast.
In Lithuania no trace remained of those
who didn't escape. Here, in America,
they'd know where their dead rested.

Twenty immigrants gathered
at the still-barren family plot.
When the first year passed without a death,
they came to celebrate,
walking through cemetery gates
to find the site and set covered baskets
down in high grass, on a slight rise.

The blanket spread on top of empty graves,
Miril and Razel make up plates
so each one gets a little of everything,
roast beef, kugel, beets; even Morris
who hates herring has to have a taste, as Ehteleh,
strong and only small because she's young,
tilts her face to feel the sun and prances
around her parents like a little goat . . .

until Jacob drives them home at dusk
and Miril sings, so the goat will dance her girl to sleep.

HARVEY M. PLOTNICK

Jewish

My skin is white, but my name is foreign, a dark inflection. I worship an unforgiving God, as outworn as His Bible, and my blood changes all human qualities to the demonic. The schoolboy forced to sing Christmas carols, I am the man who forgets the national anthem. I resemble you, but I am the false butterfly, a clone betrayed by my gait, which is racial, and my love for money, above that for my own kind. Conspiring against you, unsaved by Jesus, I am barred from your heaven forever.

But you know that you lie about me, and hatred stains your Bible (the part added to mine, both of which you call yours), and sometimes you shudder as I stir in mass graves.

A. POULIN, JR.

Red Clock

I can hear it hum in silence.
Someone nailed his heart up on my wall,
ran out, and left me with his life.

LAWRENCE RAAB

Being a Monster

Being a monster, he merely wished
to assuage his loneliness.
> —Kobo Abe

You talk about disappointment,
the insinuating perfume of the last woman
to leave you. Or the day your life
seemed to hang by a thread
anyone could snap. But no one did.
It isn't that easy to feel convinced
every part of the world can be used
against you. That loneliness,
real loneliness, won't ever desert you.
That it changes into a kind of comfort.
You tell your friends you live surrounded
by the logic of terrible mistakes.
And listening to yourself think
is another way of losing hold.
But it's not. Trust me. That's what I know,
living where I've always lived, inside
this body you'd tremble to imagine.
Which is why you want to imagine me
and tremble. To feel certain
that you and I share almost nothing.

BIN RAMKE

Paul Verlaine at the Grave of Lucien Létinois

... his grave was conceded to him for ten years. The concession was
not renewed, and presumably his bones were then thrown away.
—Joanna Richardson, *Verlaine*

What does the world with its lung of ocean breathe
if not our pale and fetid dust? We have friends
and we love more than is good for us. A decade
is time enough to forget the other things we did:
a small attempt at murder—amateurish, *mon amour*—
revives the mind admirably ...

that was the other one, my Arthur. But if you
were not my *grande passion* you were my best. The loss
of money meant the loss of your sweet bones
— you do forgive me—while his I still wear
red and clotted in my skin. I
am too ugly to grieve this way:

this picture is not pretty beneath the trees
beside the wound of earth, reopened, the grave
of someone no longer you. You knew my wounds
and wore them well.

I can, Lucien, still write:
that would please you. I recite for dinners
and for drinks. Mainly for drinks. The century wears
to a ragged close. They will forgive you,
they will forget you—your dust ultimately dissolved—
as they should.
They will watch my grave
over their left shoulders;

they will read my poems
like gambling debts, thinking:

they are pretty now;
that face is gone;
and when his only friend
died young,
he could not buy his bones.

BARBARA RAS

In the New Country

I love America. Ham bones and shoes.
Gaslight in the tenement so I can crochet
long after the sun sets with the thread
I carried out of the mill under my clothes,
out of the huge rooms of loom after loom, their beat
and thwack rattling the walls of high windows, more glass
than I saw in my eighteen years in Miadziol.
Let the women talk of the old country,
its gypsies and snakebites, the weekend fiddlers
in the warm months, always the boys
who promised ribbons.
I remember. The long winters without baths,
digging branches that didn't belong to us
out of the snow, how in the early spring
when even the potatoes were gone we ate kasha for weeks,
slept the uneasy sleep of the hungry, dreaming of cream
from many cows, its taste changing from day to day,
animal to animal.
Let them say the rye was sweeter.
I remember the bitter of no bread.

This is America. Look at this photograph:
my husband and I seated, our three children
standing around us. Under my dress I'm wearing stockings
that I unrolled carefully with gloves on my hands.
My children know English. Why look back?
I know where my father and mother are buried,
how in one month they left me with little brothers
and nothing else but to marry. You ask about love?
We saw the ocean for the first time crossing

all its waters. My children were born here, the first
on Ellis Island, and I was not afraid.
Everyone was wearing shoes.
Here my youngest can ask horrified if anyone
would eat a rabbit. There is food—breakfast, lunch, and supper.
Cabbage year round. We have respect.
When my middle child sings at the table,
my husband hits her with a spoon.
After we eat, the oldest takes the wagon
around to the neighbors, collecting scraps
we'll feed to the pig in the cellar.

C. L. RAWLINS

Living in at least two worlds

Back from the spring in the green draw
packing water, galvanized pail half-full
bells against the doorframe, slops,
(limestone water's sweet, granite water pure).
Stove rumbles, holding fire; spilled drops
roll like a busted string of pearls on hot, black iron.
Out back, four horses genuflect and sniff
at the tight-latched oat-box lid. Life.

Radio sings with a woman's voice,
the song ends, I flip a cake,
watching the first sunbeam
strike a map of mountains, head south
down the line-shack wall.

Forty miles to the Boulder Store
on a road nobody likes after the first trip.
Regular as church: eggs, coffee, cheese,
apples, flour, rice, beans. Cartons
in the pickup bed, wedged with care.
Beer with Grant or Doc or Norm:
whoever got bucked off or too damn wet to bale.

Read letters in the truck. No one
I asked can come: work, school, new loves,
Alaska, France, New Zealand,
anyplace but here. I buy more beer.

Eleven thousand bumps and I'll be back,
left, left, right, and the road forgets
at a boulderpile the glacier dropped.

I pop the gate loop, drive through, stop.
The horses dust up, woof, wheel,
nip and buck and fart,
glad the Oat-Man's home.

Big Sandy Opening, Wyoming

LIAM RECTOR

David's Rumor

for Dave Wale

I am busy doing drawings
    for the upcoming publication
Drawings of Schizophrenics in Closed Institutions.
I am busy doing drawings
    for the upcoming publication
Drawings of Schizophrenics in Closed Institutions
    because angelic voices will sing
    if I draw lost enough to listen

    and because it quiets the doctors down
    since they are anxious
    to see the book published
    and to have my efforts included. . . .

If I could find the right line, I could balance my entire design.

    Not everyone has a career,
    but the doctors have one, each of them,
    and the publication of the book *should* help to secure

    that section of their lives.

Alice, across the hall, is doing
a goodbye drawing. The doctors
are wary of this impulse
on her part, noting that Alice
says goodbye
too often. They encourage her to talk
of her plans, should she be released,

or of her past,
should she end up staying.
Alice tells them it's a "picnic,
a picnic in a light drizzle."

Here in the hospital Alice,
who killed Frank, crosses the hall each night
into my doorway and says,
"Frank, is that *you*, Frank?"

> In my drawings I omit Alice
> and concentrate
> on calling forth the hall. Schizophrenia,
> in this book, is another way of saying
> *across the hall.*

In the public room, the section where we sit and watch,
some read the newspaper while getting
the national news off the tube.
That way, if you read and listen,
you get the feeling
that the news is really coming at you,
that it might finally amount to something.

Of late I have begun to think,
I get the impression,
that our lives are being moved
by some very public rumor.

We, in darkness, picture ourselves alone
with some sort of headline: *Man Claims He Got Away
with Murder,* that sort of thing. . . .
We read as if dreaming and are then

dreamt as if living. Between
the solitary and the public, the rumor.
We picture ourselves closed-in, whirring,

but I doubt that.

In the drawings I stress
(and then surrender to) the fact
that there is some very 'hard news'
in all of us, a murderer
for each of us, and that this is how
all these reports, these *mayhems,*
finally do manage to reach us.

Pavese, the Italian, said that each
murderer is a timid suicide. Alice,
who killed Frank, wanders each night
for all of us, wondering who Frank
really is.

If I could find the right line, I could balance my entire design.

George, who lost his mind after losing
Carol, lives far down the hall. George says
Carol's infidelities at first made him want
to do away with himself, to surrender, but that later,
through the help of the doctors,
he realized it was Carol
that he wanted to kill
all along, that his impotence
was caused by a gun
that he didn't want to point
towards her, a thing he didn't want to see
go off.

None of this surprises me.
The drawings get so lost because the hall
is so wide. You come through a cauldron
before you ever sight home. . . .

My own crime bears no mention.
It was an argument, a debate gone wrong,
an affection historied into the berserk.

My work here now, my *calling,*
is to get these lines down right, to *delineate*
their deep gossip, that precise chamber
where they, right or wrong, do yak sublime. . . .

    And the doctors,
    and the doctors say the book will receive
    national distribution and I'm glad,
    yes glad with all my heart,
    for that. Ambition,
    which is finally what we do to each other,
    will undoubtedly see this project
    into its rise and quiet. . . .

And the lines go off, they wander. . . .

If I could find the right line, it could balance, balance
this riot, that hall, that vacancy and pressure
wherein we draw towards goodbye.

CARTER REVARD

Parading with the Veterans of Foreign Wars

Apache, Omaha, Osage, Choctaw, Comanche, Cherokee, Oglala, Micmac:
our place was ninety-fifth,
and when we got there with our ribbon shirts
and drum and singers on the trailer,
women in shawls and traditional dresses,
we looked into the muzzle of
an Army howitzer in front of us.
"Hey, Cliff," I said,
"haven't seen guns that big
since we were in Wounded Knee."
Cliff carried the new American flag
donated by another post; Cliff prays
in Omaha for us, being chairman
of our Pow-Wow Committee, and his prayers
keep us together, helped
by hard work from the rest of course.
"They'll move that one-oh-five ahead," Cliff said.
They did, but then the cavalry arrived.
No kidding, there was this troop outfitted
with Civil War style uniforms and carbines,
on horseback, metal clopping on
the asphalt street, and there
on jackets were the insignia:
the Seventh Cavalry, George Custer's bunch.
"Cliff," Walt said, "they think you're Sitting Bull."
"Just watch out where you're stepping, Walt,"
Cliff said, "Those pooper-scoopers
will not be working when the parade begins."
"Us women walking behind the trailer

will have to step around it all
so much, they'll think we're dancing,"
was all that Sherry said.
We followed
the yellow line, and here and there
some fake war-whoops came out to us
from sidewalk faces, but applause
moved with us when the singers started,
and we got our banners seen announcing
this year's Pow-Wow in June,
free to the public in Jefferson Barracks Park—
where the Dragoons were quartered for the Indian Wars.
When we had passed the Judging Stand
and pulled off to the little park all
green and daffodilly under the misting rain,
we put the shawls and clothing in the cars
and went back to the Indian Center, while
Cliff and George Coon went out and got
some chicken from the Colonel
that tasted great, given the temporary
absence of buffalo here in the
Gateway to the West, St. Louis.

MARTHA RHODES

Why She Hurries Out, Then Home

She's always expecting disaster,
blood scribbled on walls,
an empty carcass hung from a lamp,
roof and bricks collapsed, all she owns
shredded and burnt.
                              Watching others' children
on their way to school,
stiff in their snowsuits,
reach to hug their parents goodbye,

she hurries out, then home,
counts the blocks, forces her hands
in her pockets (everyone's safe, she is safe).

She's always resisting what's criminal in her,
a small gray cloud waiting at the gate.

DAVID RIVARD

Summons

Suppose I can convince myself this
world is my home only by claiming it
could never be & then assuming we all
share that feeling, a bond which anchors us
each to the planet, even those hired
to populate this photo, spread across
pages twenty-four & twenty-five, a beach
party, & the magazine scented because
what else should summon us to delusion
but perfume, drifting up from the tanned
and fiercely healthy faces, a massaged glow,
in precise attunement to the means
implied by the Queen Anne porch & gables,
women in summer evening dresses, barefoot,
heels tossed in clumps of eel grass, lightly
wavering stalks, & two men in tuxes
about to heap driftwood atop a bonfire
while a third lugs the straw hamper of food
and wines, the models' laughter unheard
but booming out over dunes & waves,
joyful efflorescent laughing, easy to envy,
and hidden inside their shouts another shot
of them, later, clothes stripped off, drunken,
running down the beach into a warm
plankton-lit surf, since these are the seas
out of which we once evolved crawling
and skittering over one another's backs.

LEN ROBERTS

The Assignment

All of the pens leaked
and the pencils had no
    points,
the paper crinkled from
dark days of the weekend
    spent
in the cavern of my desk,
and yet I was to write
a hundred words in perfect
    script
that Monday morning about
how I spent my weekend,
with a drawing permitted
    at the end
Looking out the window
from my last seat in the
    last row
of that fifth-grade class
I saw my brother's duck-ass
    gleaming
in the Friday night mirror,
the glimmer of his change,
gold watch, black onyx ring
    on the table,
I heard my mother sobbing
in the dark bedroom, the
    absence
of my father in his usual
    rocking

chair, knowing even then
Sister did not want to hear
the words my mother yelled,
the words my brother yelled
    back,
feel the cold of upstate New
    York
when the door opened and closed,
that she did not want to walk
    slowly
into the bedroom in my slippered
    feet,
that she did not want to feel
    my mother's
heavy white arm wrap around my
    neck
until it was all I could do to
    hold
up my head, that the words my
    mother
whispered into my ear were not
    words
Sister wanted to hear, each one
    so soft,
so distinct, both of us knowing
    there was no
where to run or hide in that house,
    that
it would be hours before my father
staggered home from Boney's Bar.

ALANE ROLLINGS

For Dear Life

> We thought we would be at sea for three days at most.
> —Pedro Gamez

Before we pushed off for Moon in Mañana land,
we watched the rain from twig-and-blanket tents on Cuba's beaches.
Hundreds of empty rafts rose and fell in the azure swell.
One by one, they heaved off, overloaded,
and were swallowed up by the curve of the earth.
    Some who sailed came floating back, mud in their mouths,
fish in their trousers, and moving their eyes as if alive.
    What a way of Nowhere! As if a raft with a mast

could improve our agony!
    I'd thought we were all relatives.
We had gods for the helpless, since there was no help for them,
also no medicine, work, or money, only the hungry
to feed the hungry, and the common, honorable desperation.
    When we fell on the picked remains of a pig some outsider
        had stolen,
we called the outcast one of us,
the theft legitimate.

    An ocean away from Florida, even walking isn't free.
    The sun is twenty feet above me; sweat is steaming
from my skin; my eyes leak ocean.
    Lost beneath a sky that birds can figure and divide,
we finish our milk and signal with mirrors, flares, our shirts.
Sharks circle; I gnaw my belt; I suck my lip so I don't drink
the ocean that we're tossed upon. Do we get to live our lives
or do they get lived for us?

How we've waited to be welcome!
Starving, we bound down the gangplank. They ask who we are that
    we're starving
and send us back up to go elsewhere.
    Where? Oh God! It's Nowhere!
    Guantànamo, Cuba, a refugee camp with khaki tents, a video store,
two loudspeakers with Cuban music, laundromats, razor wire,
and very little water. "Paradise." We have to pray
they let us die right here for the rest of our lives.

    In disbelief they'd sail for nothing,
and in faith the world awaits them,
boats are loading now in China. Don't they hear us shouting "Miami!"?
I won't wrap *my* skin around their disembarking skeletons.
    I want to tell America the Beautiful my *own* raft stories:
how the sea, riled at being second-guessed,
chewed my hopes and spit them in my face mixed with vomit
no wind would take away;

how thirst turned to pain;
how each of us bled and prayed only for himself,
held on for dear life or whatever it would take
to get out of it, or get let in at last.
    So here we are, holding on by anger, hunger, wonder that we're still
holding on, having crossed an ugly gulf to be back as we began:
scavenging—though it's *our* bones that have been sucked of marrow—
hoping

we won't be combing Nowhere for those bones
before the degradation's over.
    Now and then, we catch them hating us; they catch us holding
everything they own against them. It's not fate; it just happens.

One lacks; the other clutches. One pulls back;
the other clings.

    We have no choice in that: we're still here, here, here
in this mess of a sea that never settles.

WENDY ROSE

Long division: A tribal history

Our skin loosely lies
across grass borders;
stones loading up
are loaded down with placement sticks,
a great tearing
and appearance of holes.
We are bought and divided
into clay pots; we die
on granite scaffolding
on the shape of the Sierras
and lie down with lips open
thrusting songs on the world.
Who are we and do we
still live? The doctor,
asleep, says no.
So outside of eternity
we struggle until our blood
has spread off our bodies
and frayed the sunset edges.
It's our blood that gives you
those southwestern skies.
Year after year we give,
harpooned with hope, only to fall
bouncing through the canyons,
our songs decreasing
with distance.
I suckle coyotes
and grieve.

VERN RUTSALA

Shame

This is the shame of the woman whose hand hides
her smile because her teeth are bad, not the grand
self-hate that leads some to razors or pills
or swan dives off beautiful bridges however
tragic that is. This is the shame of being yourself,
of being ashamed of where you live and what
you father's paycheck lets you eat and wear.
This is the shame of the fat and the old,
the unbearable blush of acne, the shame of having
no lunch money and pretending you're not hungry.
This is the shame of concealed sickness—diseases
too expensive to afford that offer only their cold
one-way tickets out. This is the shame of being ashamed,
the self-disgust of the cheap wine drunk, the lassitude
that makes junk accumulate, the shame that tells
you there is another way to live but you are
too dumb to find it. This is the real shame, the damned
shame, the crying shame, the shame that's criminal,
the shame of knowing words like "glory" are not
in your vocabulary though they litter the Bibles
you're still paying for. This is the shame of not
knowing how to read and pretending you do. This is
the shame that makes you afraid to leave your house,
the shame of food stamps at the supermarket when
the clerk shows impatience as you fumble with the change.
This is the shame of dirty underwear, the shame
of pretending your father works in an office
as God intended all men to do. This is the shame
of asking friends to let you off in front of the one

nice house in the neighborhood and waiting
in shadows until they drive away before walking
to the gloom of your house. This is the shame
at the end of the mania for owning things, the shame
of no heat in winter, the shame of eating cat food,
the unholy shame of dreaming of a new house and car
and the shame of knowing how cheap such dreams are.

IRA SADOFF

Nazis

Thank God they're all gone
except for one or two in Clinton Maine
who come home from work
at Scott Paper or Diamond Match
to make a few crank calls
to the only Jew in New England
they can find

These make-shift students of history
whose catalogue of facts include
every Jew who gave a dollar
to elect the current governor
every Jew who'd sell this country out
to the insatiable Israeli state

I know exactly how they feel
when they say they want to smash my face

Someone's cheated them
they want to know who it is
they want to know who makes them beg
It's true Let's Be Fair
it's tough for almost everyone
I exaggerate the facts
to make a point

Just when I thought I could walk to the market
just when Jean the check-out girl
asks me how many cords of wood I chopped
and wishes me a Happy Easter
as if I've lived here all my life

Just when I can walk into the bank
and nod at the tellers who know my name
where I work who lived in my house in 1832
who know to the penny the amount
of my tiny Jewish bank account

Just when I'm sure we can all live together
and I can dine in their saltbox dining rooms
with the melancholy painting of Christ
on the wall their only consolation
just when I can borrow my neighbor's ladder
to repair one of the holes in my roof

I pick up the phone
and listen to my instructions

I see the town now from the right perspective
the gunner in the glass bubble
of his fighter plane shadowing the tiny man
with the shopping bag and pointy nose
his overcoat two sizes too large for him
skulking from one doorway to the next
trying to make his own way home

I can see he's not one of us

SHERYL ST. GERMAIN

Cajun

I want to take the word back into my body, back
from the northern restaurants with their neon signs
announcing it like a whore. I want it to be private again,
I want to sink back into the swamps that are nothing
like these clean restaurants, the swamps
with their mud and jaws and eyes that float
below the surface, the mud and jaws and eyes
of food or death. I want to see my father's father's
hands again, scarred with a life of netting and trapping,
thick gunk of bayou under his fingernails,
staining his cuticles, I want to remember the pride he took
gutting and cleaning what he caught; his were nothing
like the soft hands and clipped fingernails that serve us
in these restaurants cemented in land, the restaurants nothing
like the houses we lived and died in, anchored in water,
trembling with every wind and flood.

And what my father's mother knew:
how to make alligator tail sweet, how to cut up
muscled squirrel or rabbit, or wild duck,
cook it till it was tender, spice it and mix it all up
with rice that soaked up the spice and the game so that
it all filled your mouth, thick and sticky, tasting
like blood and cayenne. And when I see the signs
on the restaurants, *Cajun food served here,*
it's like a fish knife ripping my belly, and when I see
them all eating the white meat of fat chickens

and market cuts of steak or fish someone else
has caught cooked *cajun style,* I feel it
again, the word's been stolen, like me,
gutted.

KALAMU YA SALAAM

Name the Oldest Member of Your Family

the baby, the newborn, is the oldest
member of the family, not yet fully a person
her whole being is ancient, albeit fresh
into the contemporary air she is a bundle
of chromosomes & flesh drawn from every forebear who
preceded her bawling in this world, in her bones
she knows nothing but the impulses of spirits
this society misnames ghosts, she will put
a block, her hand, a rose, a roach into her mouth
attempting to taste everything, and as she grows
she will become younger until she is so old
on the threshold of death, the thinness of her skin
a translucent veil parting in preparation for her transition,
her descent into the depths of resurrection, a total dissolving
into the body of the earth, and her ascension into the bodies
of progeny, the common faraway look of elders
which we mistake for some sentimental remembering
is really the twilight savoring of the delectable
newness of every precious breathing moment, the flavor
that normally only those just entering or just leaving
eternity are wise enough to distinguish

NICHOLAS SAMARAS

Mute Prophets

There is a language before
no language but a cry,
an implication of speech
before the words become
smaller, complete, gone.

Nine hundred years ago,
the world knew Stylites,
black-robed men who lived
on high pillars, divorcing
the earth, civilization
at shoulder-height,
the level of human discourse.
Unafraid of heights but observant
of widths, they mouthed
words heavenward, drank rain,
ate small food lifted in baskets,
carried the legend of silence
with the littered world
crumbling noisely below—
until a squalid Empire forced
a holy man down from his perch,
to step out on his faith,
scorching the land and court air
with his mere presence
until the emperor himself
begged the wordless elder
to return to his altitude

and let the world continue
in circumspection.

In their way, the mute
still shake the world.
Our time is an old time.
Soon, what prophets we have
will stop speaking.
And the world
will tremble.

JAY SCHNEIDERS

Weight

All day long she works *to not feel fat*. She culls,
lessens what she weighs, imagining the heart is stone.
She mills, doubting—rises over earth. As dust. Broken
harvest grass on wind. Lithe, above road.

Tonight a man wants her to feel all the way through skin.
And if she comes, she knows she'll hate him for getting her
to know this about herself:
                              tenderness is unfamiliar.

He moves like a tractor over rough land. When he touches her
arms, she wants to smile. He is watching her smile. And there
is something they both know now: The feeling of walking
for days not riding in the car. Then riding in a car again.

Her skin ripples: rain pricking the surface of still water.
Sex is wet everywhere
                            wet, men lap at the jutting rock,
women gurgle, pool the tides.

She arches her fat back to the psalm on his tongue. Shy
women everywhere within her draw out the appoggiatura, extend the
    line.
She takes time to recall songs of another man who took her years ago,
launching birch canoe into boundary waters, an old still night.

Now he moves into forest, cares only about forest, and she finds herself
stumbling after him, willing to be there
                                    for days, floating the runoff
    and the spill,
everywhere the rotted split roots run the soil, fill with rain.

When she returns, her skin breaks space with him. But the harvest land
does not cooperate. She swarms with bees, and how do you stop it
if you want it to go on and on? She needs to find a piano, write a story,
place toast in front of a quiet man.

She is never home, never quite all the way home. Now, even for the lies
he tells her kissing her eyes, holding her face like handsful of water,
she believes that this will happen again soon.

                                    But nothing will ever happen

like this. We are all wilderness,
wild when we take to another's arms,
forgetting later there are moments
we would have it no other way.

GRACE SCHULMAN

New Netherland, 1654

Pardon us for uttering a handful
of words in *any* language, so cut loose
are we from homes, and from His name that is still
nameless, blessed be He. We raised a prayer house—

that is, we broke new wood for one, but some
tough burned it, snarling: "Carve only stones for the dead."
Damp ground, no fire, no psalm we all remember.
But tall ships anchor here, and at low tide,

people with wheat-colored hair look out to sea,
just as we'd searched for land. "Pray if you must,"
my father said, "and when prayer fails, a story—
if it is all you have, will do." Months past,

we left Recife's force-worship laws in the Year
of *their* Lord, sixteen hundred and fifty-four, for our new
world, old-country Amsterdam. Leagues seaward,
Spanish pirates slaughtered our scant crew,

and all that was left of us (friends wheezed
their last while they ragged us on) rose up on deck
and tossed our bags in the sea. We watched the wake
turn silver: kiddush wine cups, hanging bowls,

a candelabra for the promised altar,
carved pointers. Books' pages curled and sank,
prayer shawls ballooned, and, soaking, spiraled downward.
Just as we stared, again we heard swords clank—

a French ship, the Ste. Catherine (her prow had shone
gold on a gray horizon) came to our

port side and rescued us. In that commotion
on deck, we crouched below—not out of fear,

I swear, but stunned by luminous words
that echoed oddly—beautifully—like lightning
flickering through palls of thickset clouds.
A jaunty captain rasped to us in hiding:

"Where are you bound?"
                              "Amsterdam. Old country."
"Where?"
              "Amsterdam."
                              "Antilles?"
                                        "No, Amsterdam."
"Yes, yes. Nieuw *Am*sterdam. I'll see
you get there safely." He meant well, bless him.

Ste. Catherine sailed to land at its tip no larger
than a meadow, fanned out at its sides:
Manhattan Island. Our new master,
Stuyvesant, lashed us with phrases, *wheffs, guzzads,*

that stung but were not fathomed, mercifully,
when we came on a Sabbath, more than twenty
men, women, a baby born at sea.
Still cursing, he let us land, and heard our praise,

then disappeared among lank citizens
with faded skin who stride to the bay and brood
on water that we trust and dread, and listen
to tales unstamped by laws and never sacred.

JAMES R. SCRIMGEOUR

Lines Started Outside Filene's Basement

on the second floor of the Worcester Center Mall, 7:15 P.M., March 3,
1991, while waiting for my wife and her sister to try on dresses and
looking over the mostly deserted stores, at the chain curtains let down
so the merchandise (what's left of it) cannot get out—thinking of the
clerks behind bars in their darkened stores counting their meager take
while I'm sipping my ice and diet soda from Orange Julius (the only
other store open) instead of coffee, which the attendant had warned me
off of saying: "It's pretty bad. It's been sitting around for a while," all else
closed, even Jordan Marsh, the increasingly barren, sinking flagship
with its 40% off, Going Out Of Business sale—watching every once in a
while a person going up or down the escalator, an eerie, quiet depressing
depression scene overall, everything in decline, even

the fountain appears tired, worn out, only half
its lights on, the emerging water forms:
puny gurgling hunchbacked wraiths
halfheartedly attempting to escape,—

                                        being interrupted
by the well-dressed middle-aged man with the slight British accent asking
me for a match (which of course I don't have) no light, no connection to
the black teen with his baseball cap on backwards and his back to the
fountain while facing the square of light that is Filene's Basement and
inhaling his cigarette—feeling no connection to the young white with
the scruffy beard who wanted to stay but left with the fat hispanic
woman who said: "I'm going!" and meant it! "What's up, Jack?" he
offered in passing "Not much" I replied as friendly as I could, "Nice
hat!" he said, already passed, "Thanks," I replied to his receding shape—
and thinking the parking costs $10.00 to get into this place.

PETER SEARS

The One Polar Bear

You know how in the zoo most of the polar bears
look good—big, white, eating and lying around,
and when a polar bear stands up, wow! And there's
one polar bear by itself. Look closely, you can
see its coat worn in spots to the bone, sores
the size of plates. The bear lumbers to the bars
and rubs, right on the sores. Sure they get worse!
And you can see the sores getting worse, redder
and bigger. The attendants, can they do anything
about it? Ask them. Nothing works. Nothing
makes the bear happy. You know why? The bear
doesn't want to be happy. Maybe the bear
doesn't even want to be a bear, be anything.
I know about rubbing yourself away on the bars.

TIM SEIBLES

Manic: A Conversation with Jimi Hendrix

—Berkeley, California August 1970

All these hang-ups, all this time wasted when
everything really could be really groovy. I mean
I'm not tryin to come down on anybody, you know,
but the whole thing is a big, fat comedown—
nobody think I notice that almost all my audience
is mostly white. Man, I'm not blind and I can't   I mean
music isn't about whether your skin, how your skin is.
Music is somebody arguing with God. It's about
what you feel about bein alive,
here, right now: Vietnam to the left of you—
Watts to the right   and straight ahead, the future
like a really beautiful girl whose face you can't
quite make out—maybe 'cause you're scared, maybe
'cause you're so busy pretending, so wrapped up
in cellophane   you forget to unzip your heart.

We can't go on livin like this, and anyway, you can tell
the world is begging for a change—where you're loved
for who you are   instead of for what you got from Sears
and whoever. Ever since the beginning of America
they been sellin us this idea that buying things
make you a better person, but it just make you a slave—
them things you got **got you**   as much as you got them.
You're workin every day without a minute to make love in,
tryin to pay for all your pretty wall-to-wall rugs
and fur this and leather that, knowin all the time
your life is zoomin by in one a'them *wish-I-had-a* cadillacs.

  And all this bad electricity between the races—
  I think alotta people, well everybody, everybody,

well almost everybody is tired a' bein afraid
and then actin like their fear is really hate
and then hurting people which just causes more fear
and hate and on and on down the yellow brick road
to where you can't even say hello to a body
unless they're your mother and lord knows
you better not **love** nobody of another shade.

I mean, what kind of life is that—*I would love you,*
but you're too dark, you're too light, you're
too beige? I mean, here we are, all of us, ridin
on the back of this huge, iridescent dragonfly
called Earth   and all we can think, the best we can do
is keep comin up with new ways to make it impossible
to live together. Even the devil gotta be amazed
at how we're tearin ourselves apart—more in love
with money than with people. So sad, so sad.

But at the same time alotta people are lazy.
All they wanna do is be angry.
They don't try to **become** something new—
which is the only way the world ever really changes.
If we keep runnin around with all these sledgehammers,
and all the governments do is send in more pigs,
man, it's just gonna be a big mess.
And music has got to help. Definitely.
The music has got to become a new religion.
All these *thou-shalts* and *you-better-nots*
hasn't gotten us no closer to heaven. Matter a'fact,
it's just the opposite: 90% of the people act afraid
of their bodies, scared to be naked. That
doesn't seem helpful, not at all.

Our bodies are a hundred percent natural.
You don't see nobody puttin boxer shorts on zebras.
But that's all part of the pretense: if you keep
your pinstripe suit on you can play like
you're not part of the jungle. Without your body
you're not here, man. Like God ain't got nothin
better to do than be bashful. Like the Pope
all buried in curtains: we don't need him. What kind
of example is that? The music has got to teach
that **anybody** can be Jesus—woman or man—but
that's like the *M&M* candy thing, you know,
melts in your mouth, not in your hand: talkin
is not enough. I've gotta push a little
love and understanding **in sound.**

I wanna play for everybody—Chinese, people in
Nigeria—but I still don't consider myself *ambitious.*
Seem like such a military term   and we don't need
no more soldiers. We need to cut down on dyin.
Once upon a time I was s'posed to be a paratrooper.
I was in the army and everything, but I got hurt
on a practice jump. Some leprechaun reached up,
twisted my ankle and saved my behind.
When they get you in a uniform you become capable
of some very scary things, man—like who was born
to *take orders?* Who jumps out of a plane
just to land in a scene where people want to shoot you?

Don't get me wrong: we're all just babies down here—
even soldiers   but somebody flips you into *your country,*
some goat-eyed general draws some lines on a map,
next thing you know you're in *their country,*

in their jungle, lickin somebody's blood
off your bayonet. But I try to stay positive,
play loud like a baby cryin for his mama. But damn,
even at Woodstock you're not sure they can hear you,
like maybe nobody can dig why you're up there
fussin with the strings, searchin for those notes
that make you more than entertainment. Sammy Davis
is cool   so's Frank Sinatra, but a guitar solo
can be a sermon—know what I mean?

Most of the time I just can't do it
and I get so mad, but some days, like
at Rainbow Bridge, everything comes: the beach
right behind the stage, the green-blue sea,
gallons of grape wine and grass, no tickets, no
pigs, no buttons to push, and we made a music that day
that made at least one angel glad—there was this breeze
like ostriches   like ostrich feathers
being drug over you again and again—
now who do you think was behind that?

And all that day, man, nobody died. You might think
I'm losin my mind, but I had this feeling all day
that **nobody** in the whole world died—ol' man Death
was spendin the weekend in some other Milky Way.
And that's how it should be. I mean, I believe music
can save people   because most a'the time people
die too easy, like they're already halfway gone
and any little nudge sends'em right to the next world.
Good music can remind you why it's, why livin
is such magic. Well, I guess if you watch the,
"The Wild Kingdom" sometimes, after'while

you might have your doubts, but when I go,
they gonna have to pry me loose from here,
dig me out witta steam shovel—at least,
that's the way I feel about it now. Later on,
I might get really tired of all this and just
drift downstream   or I could just disappear, zap!
like some bug snatched by a bullfrog.
Or I might take it to another level, slip into
Sherwood Forest   turn into a Cheshire Cat—
you know   a *Hendrix In Wonderland* type a'thing,
which could be really outtasight when you think about it,
you know   just a smile—all that's left of you
is a smile, you know.

MYRA SHAPIRO

To Jerusalem, 1990

1. To Jerusalem

It's a *sheroot*, that's what
Israelis call a jitney, a car for hire,
layering nine people—more—in tiers,
our baggage rope-tied overhead
like the upper layer in a dig,
the jumble of us a somehow-

linked-together carload underneath.
Three Harredim (black coats, black hats)
insist on sitting separate;
they climb in back. No smile, no greeting,
they want no part of me, a woman,
no wig or scarf to hide my hair.

One holds a little girl on his lap
whispering to her from time to time,
not in Hebrew but in Yiddish:
Mameleh, du vilst shpillen?—
language of my childhood, labials that cling
like steamed milk to its cup.

So when the man who coos the child
tells the others where he lives is good—
you don't see any gentiles, you don't see
any dirt—*me zet nit kayn goy,
me zet nit kayn shmutz*—I burn.
He means my son-in-law

is filth, my daughter's love
is unacceptable. In sounds that sing

257

he spits. This is the homeland, we
are related, but home, he says, is his.
There it is—Jerusalem—suddenly
on its hill—and I am not prepared.

2. Gaza

The Story

"It was at the time when boys begin to play volleyball—about two
hours after noon. At three, when soldiers circle in their trucks on the
other side of the barricade, some boys near the game picked up stones,
to throw them. Then one soldier stood on the shoulders of the other
to be above the barrels. All the boys ran. But this boy was last—his
friends yelled *run, run*—but this boy wanted to pick up his volleyball
and suddenly the shot—the others heard it, saw the nose of a rifle
through the crack of the barrels. Everyone stayed away from the boy
bleeding from the back of his neck, his mouth, afraid if they ran to
him." His cousin is telling the story. Outside, in the alley, boys chant
Allah Akbar, Allah Akbar. A doctor sitting near the father speaks; he
has examined the X-ray, the plastic bullet. The father stares, body
sunk in his windbreaker.

The Home

Thirty men sit against four walls
where four of us have entered. Unsweetened
coffee comes round. The father,
looking nowhere, sits, young father
in his blue windbreaker. Bundled grey
the grand-uncle, in perfect English,
lifts his voice. Tremulous:
"A fourteen-year-old, an innocent—see him—
(a picture of a dark-haired boy

passes to face us—the fringed black and white
kaffiyah draping his shoulders, the smile,
his dark eyes) murdered. Could they
not have aimed for his feet, his legs,
his ass? but to aim for his head . . ."
He touches my knee as if to punctuate
each plea. "Are we animals with tails hanging
they chase us? We love, we cry.
Yet I speak to live in peace with you—we are
brothers." His voice ascends, his cheeks go red.
Tears make his eyes glow.
I know this is real life but I think
we are in *The Merchant of Venice.*

3 The King David Hotel

Graceless, yellow stone facade
stout as a matron, as a safe.
This is where history takes place,
where the British headquartered,
where tea and cushy sofas, scrolled
Byzantine designs and French doors
lead beyond to the stone veranda
where Paul Newman stood, Ari
in *Exodus,* blue-eyed and Jewish
and brave, citadel of the old city
at his back, image across oceans
and continents, projected over
and over at the Wink Theater
in a Georgia town where my father
found work, where children
my age (Jack Benny, Betty G.)

never lived next to Jews, and
their mother first day ran her hands
through my hair for horns I never
heard of. Someone called *Killer,*
so Miss Pipkin tells the third grade
Jesus was a Jew. That's history. Today
I am here, I am raising the King David
cup from the table, lifting my fork
to a petit-four glazed in blue sugar, just as
I ate with the doll I named Gloria, alone
after school, in my own house. Home.

DON SHARE

Divorced

The air is swimming with the bugs' forlorn Morse code on a hellish
    mid-morning;
Lakewater spitting at us with each choppy oar-splash;
Boys in baseball caps on passing shells who return no greetings;
Arthur yelling unintelligible insults about my J-stroke;
Jane in the bow shovelling water fiercely in all the wrong directions;
Brick factory buildings clogging the banks of the seedy Charles from
    Newton to Waltham;
Culverts, water-lilies, water-bottles, branches, rope and sun-sparkle
    making me afraid to drown;
An old woman pausing in slow surprise on an overpass as she sees
    us thrashing;
The sun moving with no visible circumference, the sky flat, cloudless,
    high;
The wind insistent, our rhythm inconstant, my thoughts divorced.

JASON SHINDER

The One Secret That Has Carried

Irene loves a man
     who is afraid of sex—
          she's attended

to everything,
     said it was okay,
          held me until I slept.

She says, *Why don't you just*
     not think about it?
          But I want to know

every sensation
     nothing untouched,
          though I pull my hand away

once she's found it.
     I can't be around a woman
          too long,

too much.
     I say, *I was mistreated.*
          She says, *a cup of tea?*

I say I can't start a thing
     and then describe the kind
          of thing I'd start.

We talk about ballrooms,
    long sleeves and sashes,
        say someday

we should go somewhere
    though we can't think
        of anywhere

and then I say abruptly,
    I've never loved
        hard enough

to be loved back.
    I say it like I've had enough
        of the whole god damn

world and will never
    be satisfied.
        I'm looking at the wall.

She's looking out the window
    because she needs
        to be somewhere.

ENID SHOMER

Falling for Jesus

For years I wanted to trade
the six-pointed star for the cross,
to enter the cool vault
of cathedrals, to tell the beads
in the dead tongue of saints,
and bear my sins like cut
flowers, fresh
for only a week at a time.

As a girl I longed for Christmas trees,
the dog tracking tinsel
through the house, all six of us kneeling
in pajamas over gift-wrapped
love. I wanted Ivory Liquid
at the kitchen sink,
not the bar of kosher soap
with its strict blue stripe.

O Easter rabbits and dyed eggs,
the white mantilla knit of snowflakes
that framed the face of my friend
Annie Palm, who entered the convent
at sixteen and stayed
for twenty-one years. With the Father
I had to remain a good girl
while with the Son she had a big brother

to take the blame.
When Annie left the Order
she hung a crucifix above her bed.
And I saw in that figure what all

the young Annies must see: the sacred
bleeding, pierced flesh, eyes closed
in a slack face—the pose
of a woman in love.

CHARLES SIMIC

The Inner Man

It isn't the body
That's a stranger.
It's someone else.

We poke the same
Ugly mug
At the world.
When I scratch,
He scratches too.

There are women
Who claim to have held him.
A dog follows me about.
It might be his.

If I'm quiet, he's quieter.
So I forget him.
Yet, as I bend down
To tie my shoelaces,
He's standing up.

We cast a single shadow.
Whose shadow?

I'd like to say:
"He was in the beginning
And he'll be in the end,"
But one can't be sure.

At night
As I sit

Shuffling the cards of our silence,
I say to him:

"Though you utter
Every one of my words,
You are a stranger.
It's time you spoke."

MARK SOLOMON

A Comment on My Host

What a relief to be speaking again, restored
    to life if only for a moment. This body I inhabit—reluctant,
      jealous host—imposes strict, unpleasant regulations.

I don't blame him. I am careless, an ungrateful guest. I leave
    beds piled with their soiled linen, dishes
      in the sink, uncovered plates in the refrigerator.
I never remember to water his plants or to feed
    his ridiculous animals. I inhabit his body
      as if it were one of my own and I had many
to spare. I leave it enervated, cranky, painfully dissatisfied.

    I refused to go to Jerusalem with him. Oh the weariness
      of sharing quarters with his holy son, wandering
narrow ancient alleys in search of scribes and prophets,
    handing out cold cash without distinction to tzaddikim
      and charlatans. I can sense the "pleasures"
of his quests and voyages, his pleas and bargainings with mighty powers,
    both within himself and in the larger universe. Flakes
      of parched unleavened cakes still lodge in the folds
of his flesh, his ears still ring with mingled wails and hallelujahs
    from the Western Wall, his blood charged with anguish
      at the resolutions he should make, the vows he is pledged
to honor, the noble purpose of his circumcision and his precious seed.

    Tiresome. His wife can't stand him in this mode. The congregation
      where he worships in his New York neighborhood finds him
insufferable, uncommunicative, withdrawn beneath the large black-
    banded tallis he acquired in B'nai B'rak. He wanders the rooms
      of his apartment, the streets and sidewalks of the city,
a displaced refugee forever banished from his true home, true

family amid the temporary shelters of the dismal plain, searching
        the faces for someone familiar, someone who has seen
what he has seen, someone who might know what he has known.
        But his loneliness is absolute, his deprivation, perfect.
        No one here even thinks of Righteous Men, or Wise Men,
Holy Men or Seers. Over there, in B'nai B'rak, in Jerusalem, he spent
        his days and nights with them. So he believed. He prayed,
        he studied, cried and sang, bared his soul, and they
encouraged him, made sense of his stammered, fractured
        Hebrew and Yiddish, gave him blessings though they wondered
        what he could return to in Amerika.

He is like a ruined man. And so, for a while, he has lent me
        his body and once again I can crudely re-establish our connection.
        I half suspect that when I leave he sniffs the linens, sips
the dregs of wine, though he shakes his head, mumbling into his beard.

MAURA STANTON

Space

Monday a boy who cannot lift
Even a hand to wave good-bye
Comes to my office with his mother.

She has pushed him in his wheelchair
As she must have bathed and dressed him,
Clipped his beard, knocked on my door.

Now he tries to speak; he sputters.
Leaning down his mother listens,
Nodding at his urgent noises.

Then she tells me that he writes
Using his teeth to punch out letters
One by one, ten hours a page.

"What is he writing?" Yes, he hears me,
Twisting his face while his eyes shine.
"Another novel," his mother says,

"Space is his setting and his theme,
Stars beyond the firmament."
So she talks on. She makes me see

At once the creature he prefers
Floating across the dreadful night,
Speechless in their metal casing,

Viewing the universe with wonder—
Silent brains, no flesh, no spine—
Amazing in their goodness, pureness.

All the while his lonely eyes
Behold us as we talk and gesture,
Mother, teacher, aliens, stones.

GERALD STERN

Diary

I am at last that thing, a stranger in my own life,
completely comfortable getting in or getting out of my own Honda,
living from five cardboard boxes, two small grips,
                  and two briefcases.

I stopped smoking, I stopped eating eggs,
                  I stopped taking elevators.
I am as good sitting on a rock or a piece of concrete
                  as I am on a padded lawn chair.
I am starting all over with a marigold, a green tomato,
                  and a string of weak-backed delphiniums.
I am putting a brown rose to my lips as if the slaughter
                  never happened.

I am a blue-moon singer, getting up on the wrong side,
taking refuge from my own bitter candor,
seeing one too many halos and one too many runaway crescents
                  and one too many cheese-shaped candles a month.
I started off mourning, I started off with a long-stringed cello
and a pinch-lipped French horn and a flowering spit-cupped trombone
and ended up with a piano and a bell and a sliding hand
and a studio falsetto and a block for a horse's clatter.

There is a cement sidewalk between the irises for my stroll
and a wire fence for my concentration.
There is a metal chair to sit on and another one to hold my tea.
I will stay for the radio blast
and the rattle of the Greek newspaper
and the scream of the jay,
and wait all day for the moon behind the chimney
and the moon above the roof,

a mixture of two cold things
in the dark light.

The steps I will take for the most part one at a time,
holding on to the rail with my right hand
and rubbing the chalk away with my left.
I will lie on the other side this time
because of the oak mirror
and drag two heavy blankets over my head
because of the cracked window.
I will choose "Dust, Dust, Dust"
for my first sleep
and "A Kiss to Build a Dream On"
for my second
and be a just man for half of my six hours
and a bastard for the other.

An American crow, a huge croaker, a *corvus*,
who caws four times, then caws five times at six
in the morning will be my thrush,
and I will turn from painted door to hanging spider to crooked
    curtain rod
to hear his song.
Nothing in either Egypt or Crete
could equal the light coming into this room
or the sound of the Greeks shouting
behind their bolted windows.
And nothing ever was—or could be—different
than my lips moving one way
and my hands another
before coming down together
for an early breakfast

and an hour or two of silent reading
before separating in front of the boxwood
and kissing goodbye over the wilted hostas
and holding on between the few late pinched tomatoes
and the whistling dove.

CONSTANCE URDANG

Portrait

Trespasser in my own house,
my own alter-ego,
I'll never catch myself.

I'd steal my own treasures:
the silver ring set with a carnelian,
the little book bound in tooled leather.

I arrange myself like an odalisque
on the model's throne
and dare them to paint me.

Some days I impersonate myself
and walk in the city
collecting wolf-whistles and propositions.

I look for myself in the supermarket
among the stout mammas
in the odor of oranges and bananas.

In a crazy-quilt of weeds
I invade my own back yard.
Not even the dog knows me.

Woman Who Weeps

Up from the valley, ten children working the fields
and three in the ground, plus four who'd slipped like fish
from a faulty seine, she wept to the priest:
    Father, I saw the Virgin on a hill,
    she was a lion, lying on her side,
    grooming her blond shoulders with her tongue.

Six months weeping as she hulled the corn,
gathered late fruit and milked the goats,
planted grain and watched the hillside blossom,
before she went to the Bishop, kissed his ring.
    Father, I saw Our Lady in a tree,
    swaddled in black, she was a raven,
    on one leg, on one bent claw
    she hunched in the tree but she was the tree,
    charred trunk in a thicket of green.

After seven years of weeping,
not as other stunned old women weep,
she baked flat bread, washed the cooking stones,
cut a staff from a sapling by the road.
The Holy Father sat in a gilded chair:
    Father, I saw Christ's Mother in a stream,
    she was a rock, the water
    parted on either side of her,
    from one stream she made two—
    two tresses loosened across her collarbone—
    until the pouring water met at her breast
    and made a single stream again—

Then from the marketplace, from the busiest stall
she stole five ripened figs

and carried her weeping back to the countryside,
with a cloth sack, with a beggar's cup,
village to village and into the smoky huts,
her soul a well, an eye, an open door.

DEREK WALCOTT

Upstate

A knife blade of cold air keeps prying
the bus window open. The spring country
won't be shut out. The door to the john
keeps banging. There're a few of us:
a stale-drunk or stoned woman in torn jeans,
a Spanish-American salesman, and, ahead,
a black woman folded in an overcoat.
Emptiness makes a companionable aura
through the upstate villages—repetitive,
but crucial in their little differences
of fields, wide yards with washing, old machinery—where people live
with the highway's patience and flat certainty.

Sometimes I feel sometimes
the Muse is leaving, the Muse is leaving America.
Her tired face is tired of iron fields,
its hollows sing the mines of Appalachia,
she is a chalk-thin miner's wife with knobbled elbows,
her neck tendons taut as banjo strings,
she who was once a freckled palomino with a girl's mane
galloping blue pastures plinkety-plunkety,
staring down at a tree-stunned summer lake,
when all the corny calendars were true.
The departure comes over me in smoke
from the far factories.

But were the willows lyres, the fanned-out pollard willows
with clear translation of water into song,
were the starlings as heartbroken as nightingales,
whose sorrow piles the looming thunderhead

over the Catskills, what would be their theme?
The spring hills are sun-freckled, the chaste white barns flash
through screening trees the vigour of her dream,
like a white plank bridge over a quarrelling brook.
Clear images! Direct as your daughters
in the way their clear look returns your stare,
unarguable and fatal—
no, it is more sensual.
I am falling in love with America.

I must put the cold small pebbles from the spring
upon my tongue to learn her language,
to talk like birch or aspen confidently.
I will knock at the widowed door
of one of these villages
where she will admit me like a broad meadow,
like a blue space between mountains,
and holding her arms at the broken elbows
brush the dank hair from a forehead
as warm as bread or as a homecoming.

THOM WARD

On Being Kicked Out of the Harold Washington Library Center
for Napping on the Floor

Above me no seraphim or nymphs,
but crew-cut men, walkie-talkies, crisp
uniforms, the tallest saying
Sir, you'll have to leave.
This room with its mahogany clock,
azure lights, dozens of new chairs
set in perfect lines, the grain
smooth as vowels. Among tables a few students
scribble notes, others thumb pages
and everywhere the smell
of fresh wax. Down four flights
we march, one in front and one
behind, past portraits of dour
Chicago fathers, frescoes splashed
with lilies and nudes, past
magazines, blunt newspapers,
the willowy librarian
hovering pictures above children, banished
from this kingdom of books,
dear James I too
have wasted my life.

ROSANNA WARREN

Max Jacob at Saint Benoît

The noonday square. Plane leaves, dust:
they scurry in heat shimmering gusts.
Even shadows rustle. The Belgians are gone.
The tiny terrier trots alone.
Max prayed here, *le grand poseur,*
salon mystic and *littérateur,*
but fourteen years, remember, that's one hell
of a pose for a Paris swell.
He had an infallible sense of scene.
See that stone soul torn limb from limb
between the devils and seraphim?
Romanesque, of course, for Max to preen
his own soul's pretty plumage here
year after tiresome dusty year.
And still, it wasn't easy. *Quel ennui!*
This flat, hot land, the sluggish Loire;
daily, nightly, daily: *prière, devoir;*
no more blue-yellow visions of Christ on the tree
(from Max's aquarelle), no more *cinémathèque*
blue movie Maries scolding *"pauvre Max"*
(to scandalize confessors),
no more dandified mystics dogging his tracks.
At Saint Benoît, just dust. The trek
to God? Beyond the crypt, it led
from boredom to boredom to prison camp bed
in Drancy. There, the Nazis let him die
—an old Jew with pneumonia—"naturally."

ELLEN DORÉ WATSON

Battered Toddler, Page B6

Sometimes grown-ups forget you're down there
on the floor with the ant traps and loose wiring.
It would be wise not to chew either one. Daddy
will wake from his stupor, Mommy will tire
of her old Sinatras. Best to forgive them now,
before it gets worse; that way you'll have some
forgiveness left for later. When they remember
they're parents, you'll have a better shot at Kix
or popsicles or Daddy's keys if they find you
wearing a funny hat instead of shredding papers
at the mail slot. If they wake and go
straight to the medicine cabinet or each other's
throats, grab a fuzzy and get scarce. Put your
tears and shrieks into the cheap blue fur.
When their eyes happen to fall on you the moment
they hate themselves the most (you can smell it),
you must play very but not too dead. Try to
leave your body in their hands—without it
you can climb to the window ledge and look out.
Just don't forget the way back inside your bruised
skin, you will need to take it with you if you find
a time to run, or tell. If they beat all the life
out of you, red dragonflies with wings half air,
half spun gold, gazillions of them, will rise up
and bear you to the warm basket waiting
beside the stove of God. Well. Whatever death
turns out to be, it will be one good mother.

CHARLES HARPER WEBB

Beggars

Each day as I leave Holiday Health Spa,
at the stoplight where I turn on Victory,
The Mother's there: frayed blue dress,
frazzled brown hair, two grubby children,
and her sign: "Homeless, Help, Please."

If three thousand cars pass every day,
and one in ten gives her a dollar,
that's a hundred-and-ten thousand per year.
For all I know, she rents the sidewalk space
and hires the kids from Central Casting.

Beggar, bum, vagrant, tramp, drifter, hobo,
vagabond, panhandler, mendicant,
derelict, bindlestiff, homeless, disabled vet—
as many names as the Inuit have for snow.
The Chinese call beggars *jadestones-drained-*

of-blood, and *plum-trees-after-fierce-wind.*
The year my family lived in Austria,
I had to cross a stone bridge lined with them—
legless, blind, harelipped, syphilitic, clawing
at me, wailing *"Groshens! Groshens!"*

The Beef Bowl on Central closed when customers
refused to run the beggar gauntlet. The cops
couldn't interfere; beggars have rights.
Most cultures have beggar gods. Slight one,
and you could be changed into a beast.

To stay human, we must help each other,
I know. Still, when a reeking bag-man barged

into the Lone Star Steak House, and snatched
at my date's prime rib, I grabbed him
by the pants and collar—was I doing this?—

and, like in Chaplin films, tossed him outside.
My date said she felt "very protected,"
and went to bed with me. But I gave
The Mother five dollars that week, and dreamed
of stones dripping green blood, and rotting plums.

BROOKE WIESE

Everyone Who Wants to Work Can

A woman at the lecture waves her hand,
says, *Everyone who wants to work
can,* and I stiffen, rein knee-jerk
anger in, untorque my face to correspond
to those around me. I arrived late. Misunderstood
of course the context. But she says it again,
and I think of John as I pan
the roomful of faces, eager, and earnestly good,
and middle-aged, and comfortable, and pink.
John is too, and likes to work. (He flew,
before he turned to wood.) But what should he do,
lately grounded with AIDS? And what does she think
Maurice should do, black as blackbirds,
and who cannot read any of these words?

EUGENE WILDMAN

The Cure

Everyone in here hates. That is why this place is called a clinic. Because we all have to be cured. The patients hate each other, hate the doctors, hate the cashiers, hate the attendants, hate themselves. Because there are not enough sickrooms, not enough waiting rooms, not enough light, not enough air, not enough ashtrays, not enough time for any person to possibly wait to be cured.

Because we have to bring our sickness to someone not like ourselves, because we have to be grateful, because we have to apologize for taking his time, because our eyes are different and we are always talking in the dark.

Because he tells us to stay in bed for a week, because the sick and the well are not alike, because his home is beautiful and his wife is spoiled, because it is not possible to stay in bed for a week, because we have to work overtime to make up the time lost waiting for *him*.

Because sickness is not in the blood. Because aureomycin is useless. Because we are tired of cheating to get ahead of sick people. Because he goes home. Because he makes love. (To *her*.) Because he makes jokes. Because he has seen us naked. Because still we are not able to keep ourselves from feeling grateful.

Because we are sweeping the floors and we are sick. Because he would stay in bed for a week. Because she would stay in bed for two weeks. Because the cashier would stay in bed for a week and we would have to wait even longer. Because therefore we always have to hope they get well.

Because the cashier hates each of us and is hated by each of us. Because we take her light. Because we take her air. Because we take her time. Because we are sick. Because she is well. Because aureomycin is useless. Because we never stay in bed for a week. Because she peers out at us from behind bars. Because she takes our clinic cards and looks at them suspiciously.

Because she asks us who we are. Because she takes the card unlovingly. Because we secretly fear she will lose our card. Because we never stop coming back. Because we dread being given someone else's card. Because we wonder how it is that *we* have to explain.

Because there are too many millions of us for a single day. Because she is exhausted from peering out all day. Because we are exhausted from peering in all day. Because when you go up to the window to give her your clinic card, and you stare at her through the bars and she stares through at you, neither of you can tell anymore which side of the bars you are on.

C. K. WILLIAMS

The Critic

In the Boston Public Library on Boylston Street, where all the bums
    come in stinking from the cold,
there was one who had a battered loose-leaf book he used to scribble
    in for hours on end.
He wrote with no apparent hesitation, quickly, and with concentra-
    tion; his inspiration was inspiring:
you had to look again to realize that he was writing over words that
    were already there—
blocks of cursive etched into the softened paper, interspersed with
    poems in print he'd pasted in.
I hated to think of the volumes he'd violated to construct his opus,
    but I liked him anyway,
especially the way he'd often reach the end, close his work with weary
    satisfaction, then open again
and start again: page one, chapter one, his blood-rimmed eyes as rapt
    as David's doing psalms.

ELIZABETH WOODY

*She-Who-Watches . . . The Names Are Prayer**

for David Sohappy

My humanness is an embellished tongue,
the bell, a yellow mouth of September's
moon beats outward. She speaks for all
the names that clang in memorial.

There is Celilo,
dispossessed, the village of neglect
and bad structure.
The Falls are faint rocks enrippled
in the placid lake of back waters.
With a sad, stone grief and wisdom
I overlook the railroad.
The tight bands rail along
the whirls of the Columbia.
Drowning is a sensation
Fishermen and their wives know of.
Men who fished son after father.
There are drownings in The Dalles,
hanging in jails and off-reservation-suicide-towns.

A Strange Land awaits
the Fishermen,
as it had for the Nez Perce, the Navajo, Cheyenne women,
those who wailed in the Long Walks,
keened open the graves of their families.
The dead children.
My Children,
with names handed down and unused.
Nee Mee Poo, Diné, Tsistsista's.

THE PEOPLE, pure in emergence.
The Immense Mother is crying.
"Human Beings,"
the word tremors in the rib cage
of hills.

The consumption of loneliness binds us.
Children lie on the railroad tracks
to die from the wail of night and spirits.
I watch for the rushing head of chaos
and flat hands grope from the cattle cars,
clamor in the swift, fresh air.
A sky is clicking through the regular slats.
The tail whips the dusty battles of the Indian Wars,
unsettling itself, nude and raw.
Celilo Falls sank unwillingly in the new trading
and everyone dissolved from the fall.

* "She-Who-Watches," is a petroglyph on the Columbia River.
Originally a Woman Chief, the last, before Coyote changed her into
rock to watch over her people and the Men Chiefs who followed
her. Celilo Falls was the longest site of habitation for Indian people,
an estimated 10,000 years. In 1956 it was sold to accommodate
The Dalles Dam on the Columbia River.

WAI-LIM YIP

In and Out of Check Points

Is the river a boundary line?
A small boat can cross it.
Is the mountain a boundary line?
A bird can fly over it.
The sky, void, cloudless, totally unblocked
Wild geese fly south, swallows fly north
Out and back
Rising with the rising sun
Resting with the resting sun
They sky, is the sky a boundary line?
The sea stretches into the sky beyond our ken.
From here, fish in large schools follow the tides to the east.
From there, fish in large schools follow the waves to the west.
The sea, is the sea a boundary line?

At the seaport, document check after document check
At the airport, verification and verification
This is no longer a question of having wings
This is no longer a question of being able to swim
This is no longer a question of language and skin color
This is no longer a question of custom and tradition
There is simply such an invisible line
Tensed there
On one side: a group of anxious people waiting
On the other side: another group of anxious people waiting

Have you not seen
People in a passionate fashion
Proclaim from a height toward the four directions:
"We are born free"?

Is the river a boundary line?
Is the mountain a boundary line?
Is the sky a boundary line?
Is the sea a boundary line?

PAUL ZIMMER

The Example

The papers on my desk out of hand,
Rampant as an unkempt lilac bush,
I think of Leonard the obscure,
A memory from an ancient summer job,
A soiled man, teeth rotten to the gums,
With hair like gray, electric shock.
He lived by his wits and last strength
In a wretched shack down by the tracks,
A man without wife, family, or language
We could understand, his smile abiding
As he sat apart from us in the truck bed.

We'd drop him off with pruners, saw,
Jug of water, and bag of day old bread
At the biggest clumps of unkempt bushes
In the parks. At day's end when we picked
Him up, he'd be sitting on the ground smoking
His broken, taped-up pipe, the bush subdued,
Trimmed to cane, tied in neat stacks
Ready for hauling. He'd pull himself wearily
Over the tailgate and sit downwind from
Our teenage wisecracks. Secretly I thought
He was amazing. Even now as I remember him,
My fingers begin riffling through stacks
Of inventories, letters, queries, reports,
Once more I lower my wild, gray head,
Smile my abiding smile and work and work.

KELLEEN ZUBICK

Evolution of Appetite

Think about St. Joan without
her title and army.
In Rouen she wanted

scx, a man's sweat,
the feeling of hands rooting
her hair. Consider her years.

Before death, Joan asked
for an onion.
It opened lips and made her

swallow and smell.
It caught her breath up,
built that ending body's

resin store. It made her
heart paddle and her skin
burn. It made her bite

slip and her vision rinse away.
It let her weep.
Think of the sure juice

sealed over the pores
where it traveled her arm.
Think of the cinched

throat—Joan—later struggling
for comfort, and the smoke,
divoting, then lifting to end.

Acknowledgments

Kim Addonizio, "Broken Sonnets" from *Many Mountains Moving* 2, no. 1. Copyright © 1998 by Kim Addonizio. Reprinted with permission from the author.

Consuelo de Aerenlund, "Cuando el tecolote canta, el Indio muere." Copyright © 1995 by Consuelo de Aerenlund. Printed with permission from the author.

Nadya Aisenberg, "Leaving Eden" from *Leaving Eden* (London: Forest Books, 1995), 11. Copyright © 1995 by Nadya Aisenberg. Reprinted with permission from the author.

Joan Aleshire, "The Double." Copyright © 1999 by Joan Aleshire. Printed with permission from the author.

Elizabeth Alexander, "Boston Year" from *The Venus Hottentot* (Charlottesville, Va.: University Press of Virginia, 1990), 44. Copyright © 1990 by the Rector and Visitors of the University of Virginia. Reprinted with permission from the author and the University Press of Virginia.

David Alpaugh, "Herbie" from *Counterpoint* (Ashland, Oreg.: Story Line Press, 1994), 18–19. Copyright © 1994 by David Alpaugh. Reprinted with permission from the author.

Doug Anderson, "Itinerary" from *The Moon Reflected Fire* (Cambridge, Mass.: Alice James Books, 1994). Copyright © 1994 by Doug Anderson. Reprinted with permission from the author. Originally published in *Massachusetts Review*.

Bob Arnold, "No Tool or Rope or Pail" from *Where Rivers Meet* (Richmond, Mass.: Mad River Press, 1990). Copyright © 1990 by Bob Arnold. Reprinted with permission from the author.

Robert Ayres, "Corporeal." Copyright © 1999 by Robert Ayres. Printed with permission from the author.

John Balaban, "Heading Out West" from *Words for My Daughter* (Port Townsend, Wash.: Copper Canyon Press, 1991), 13–14. Copyright © 1991 by

Andrea Hollander Budy, "Ellis Island, September 1907" from *Poetry* 165, no. 2 (November 1994). Copyright © 1994 by Andrea Hollander Budy. Reprinted with permission from the author.

Hayden Carruth, "Little Citizen, Little Survivor" from *Scrambled Eggs and Whiskey* (Port Townsend, Wash.: Copper Canyon Press, 1996), 100. Copyright © 1996 by Hayden Carruth. Reprinted with permission from the author and Copper Canyon Press, P.O. Box 271, Port Townsend, WA 98368–0271.

Cyrus Cassells, "Soul Make a Path Through Shouting" from *Soul Make a Path Through Shouting* (Port Townsend, Wash.: Copper Canyon Press, 1994), 17–18. Copyright © 1994 by Cyrus Cassells. Reprinted with permission from Copper Canyon Press, P.O. Box 271, Port Townsend, WA 98368–0271.

Marilyn Chin, "We Are Americans Now, We Live in the Tundra" from *Dwarf Bamboo* (Greenfield Center, N.Y.: Greenfield Review Press, 1987), 28. Copyright © 1987 by Marilyn Chin. Reprinted with permission from the author and Greenfield Review Press.

Elizabeth Claman, "Show Biz Parties." Copyright © 1999 by Elizabeth Claman. Printed with permission from the author.

David Clewell, "Poem for the Man Who Said *Shit*" from *Blessings in Disguise* (New York: Viking, 1991), 25–26. Copyright © 1991 by David Clewell. Reprinted with permission from Viking Penguin, a division of Penguin Putnam, Inc., and the author.

Lucille Clifton, "slaveships" from *The Terrible Stories* (Brockport, N.Y.: BOA Editions, Ltd., 1996), 35. Copyright © 1996 by Lucille Clifton. Reprinted with permission from BOA Editions, Ltd., 260 East Avenue, Rochester, NY 14604.

Michael Collier, "Robert Wilson" from *The Neighbor* (Chicago: University of Chicago Press, 1995), 34. Copyright © 1995 by the University of Chicago. Reprinted with permission from the author.

Billy Collins, "Going Out for Cigarettes" from *Questions about Angels* (New York: William Morrow and Company, 1991), 51–52. Copyright © 1991 by Billy Collins. Reprinted with permission from the author.

Albert Goldbarth, "The Book of Human Anomalies" from *Laurel Review* 28, no. 2 (Summer 1994). Copyright © 1994 by Albert Goldbarth. Reprinted with permission from the author.

Alvin Greenberg, "the man in the moon" from *Chelsea,* no. 60 (1996): 94–96. Copyright © 1996 by Alvin Greenberg. Reprinted with permission from the author.

John Haines, "On a Certain Field in Auvers" from *The Owl in the Mask of the Dreamer: Collected Poems of John Haines* (St. Paul, Minn.: Graywolf Press, 1993), 193–95. Copyright © 1993 by John Haines. Reprinted with permission from the author and Graywolf Press, St. Paul, Minnesota.

Forrest Hamer, "Line up" from *Call and Response* (Farmington, Maine: Alice James Books, 1995), 49. Copyright © 1995 by Forrest Hamer. Reprinted with permission from the author.

Joy Harjo, "Anchorage" from *She Had Some Horses* (New York: Thunder's Mouth Press, 1983), 14–15. Copyright © 1983 by Joy Harjo. Reprinted with permission from Thunder's Mouth Press.

James Haug, "The Tennessee Waltz" from *The Stolen Car* (Amherst: University of Massachusetts Press, 1989), 57–58. Copyright © 1989 by James Haug. Reprinted with permission from the University of Massachusetts Press.

Anita Helle, "Poem for Natalia Ginzburg." Copyright © 1999 by Anita Helle. Printed with permission from the author.

Emily Hiestand, "The Day Lily and the Fox" from *Green the Witch-Hazel Wood* (St. Paul, Minn.: Graywolf Press, 1989), 109–10. Copyright © 1989 by Emily Hiestand. Reprinted with permission from the author and Graywolf Press, St. Paul, Minnesota.

Edward Hirsch, "Song" from *For the Sleepwalkers* (New York: Alfred A. Knopf, 1981), 70. Copyright © 1981 by Edward Hirsch. Reprinted with permission from the author.

Jonathan Holden, "Saturday Afternoon, October" from *Dacotah Territory* 14 (Spring/Summer 1977): 44–45. Copyright © 1977 by Jonathan Holden.

312

Subject Index

Body

Cultural Identity

Family

Love

Mind

Mortality

Nature

Occupation

Political

Self

LAURE-ANNE BOSSELAAR's poetry collection, *The Hour Between Dog and Wolf,* was published by BOA Editions. Among other publications, her poems have appeared in the *Massachusetts Review, Ploughshares,* the *Washington Post, Luna,* and *Harvard Review.*

She lives in Cambridge, Massachusetts, with her husband, Kurt Brown, with whom she coedited *Night Out: Poems about Hotels, Motels, Restaurants, and Bars* (Milkweed Editions, 1997). She is translating contemporary American poets into French, Flemish poetry into English, and is at work on a second book of poems.

Interior design by Donna Burch
Typeset in Minion
by Stanton Publication Services, Inc.
Printed on acid-free 55# Glatfelter paper
by Bang Printing

More poetry anthologies from Milkweed Editions:

Clay and Star:
Contemporary Bulgarian Poets
Translated and edited
by Lisa Sapinkopf and Georgi Belev

Drive, They Said:
Poems about Americans and Their Cars
Edited by Kurt Brown

Looking for Home:
Women Writing about Exile
Edited by Deborah Keenan and Roseann Lloyd

Minnesota Writes:
Poetry
Edited by Jim Moore and Cary Waterman

Mixed Voices:
Contemporary Poems about Music
Edited by Emilie Buchwald and Ruth Roston

Mouth to Mouth:
Poems by Twelve Contemporary Mexican Women
Edited by Forrest Gander

Night Out:
Poems about Hotels, Motels, Restaurants, and Bars
Edited by Kurt Brown and Laure-Anne Bosselaar

Passages North Anthology:
A Decade of Good Writing
Edited by Elinor Benedict

The Poet Dreaming in the Artist's House:
Contemporary Poems about the Visual Arts
Edited by Emilie Buchwald and Ruth Roston

This Sporting Life:
Contemporary American Poems
about Sports and Games
Edited by Emilie Buchwald and Ruth Roston

Verse and Universe:
Poems about Science and Mathematics
Edited by Kurt Brown

White Flash/Black Rain:
Women of Japan Relive the Bomb
Edited and translated by Lequita Vance-Watkins
and Aratani Mariko

Milkweed Editions publishes with the intention of making a humane impact on society, in the belief that literature is a transformative art uniquely able to convey the essential experiences of the human heart and spirit.

To that end, Milkweed publishes distinctive voices of literary merit in handsomely designed, visually dynamic books, exploring the ethical, cultural, and esthetic issues that free societies need continually to address.

Milkweed Editions is a not-for-profit press.